Dictionary of Financial and Securities Terms

Securities Institute Services

PROFESSIONALISM | *INTEGRITY* | *EXCELLENCE*

Dictionary of Financial and Securities Terms

Securities Institute Services

First published in 1999 in Great Britain by
Securities Institute (Services) Limited
Centurion House, 24 Monument Street
London EC3R 8AQ, England.

Copyright © Securities Institute Services Limited 1999

All rights reserved. No part of this publication may be reproduced, stored in a retrieval system, or transmitted, in any form or by any means, electronic, mechanical, photocopying, recording or otherwise, without the prior permission of the copyright owner.

ISBN: 1 900520 96 6 Printed July 1999

While every effort has been made to ensure its accuracy, no responsibility for loss occasioned to any person acting or refraining from action as a result of any material in this publication can be accepted by the publisher or author.

Printed and bound in Great Britain by
Anthony Rowe Limited, Chippenham, Wiltshire

Foreword

The Securities Institute is the major examining body for the securities and derivatives industry, and provides a wide range of industry qualifications. It is a substantial provider of training courses and of relevant publications. It promotes, for the public benefit, the advancement of knowledge in the area of securities and investments and consults and researches in matters of public interest concerning investment in securities.

Feedback which we have received from our Members and their clients, our students and our panel of securities practitioners, has shown that there is a real need for a new dictionary of financial and securities terms. The financial services industry is dynamic and new products are continually being created. The industry is prone to the use of abbreviations and acronyms. There is a jungle of jargon which people who do not work in the industry will find hard to penetrate.

I am pleased to introduce this new dictionary which I believe will meet a real need. It is aimed at students, financial professionals and the general public – in fact, anyone who wishes to acquire a clear understanding of a defined term of reference. The dictionary is intended to give a quick, clear and straight forward definition of frequently used terms in the financial and securities industry. Also included is a comprehensive listing of abbreviations and acronyms. The dictionary aims fairly to reflect today's practices. We will keep it up to date, and will up date the definitions when necessary.

We have tried to make this dictionary as accurate as possible, but the Editor would welcome hearing from readers who wish to suggest alternative definitions or, indeed, new terms for inclusion.

We are publishing with the dictionary a free CD–ROM version of it for users to load on to their PC for easy reference at home or at work.

Geoffrey Turner
Chief Executive
23 July 1999

Thanks to Dick Hales of the Securities Industry Management Association (SIMA) who reviewed the draft dictionary on behalf of the Technical Standards Committee for the Institute.

Securities Institute

Mission Statement:

"To set standards of professional excellence and integrity for individual practitioners, and provide the means of attaining them"

Established in 1992, the Securities Institute has become the most widely respected professional body for those who work in the securities and investment industry in the UK. Membership currently totals 12,000 and is rising.

Well known around the world for developing and promoting high standards of integrity, ethics and competence in financial services, the Institute speaks with unique authority in the financial services arena. It canvasses and expresses views on a wide range of issues including City regulation and investor confidence.

By bringing together thousands of practitioners from such a diverse and complex field into a single network, the Institute leads professionalism within the financial services industry. Alongside its serious business agenda however, it also provides opportunities for Members to meet socially.

List of Abbreviations

ABI	Association of British Insurers
AGM	Annual General Meeting
ADR	American Depositary Receipt
AEX	Amsterdam Exchange
AMEX	American Stock Exchange
APACS	Association for Payment Clearing Services
APCIMS	Association of Private Client Investment Managers and Stockbrokers
APR	Annual Percentage Rate
ASB	Accounting Standards Board
ASSET	Automated System for the Stock Exchange of Thailand
ASX	Australian Stock Exchange
AUTIF	Association of Unit Trust and Investment Funds
AVC	Additional Voluntary Contribution
BACS	Bank Automated Clearing System
BBA	British Bankers' Association
BIS	Bank for International Settlements
BOLT	Bombay Stock Exchange OnLine Trading
CAC	Compagnie des Agents de Change
CAPM	Capital Asset Pricing Model
CBI	Confederation of British Industry
CBOE	Chicago Board Options Exchange
CBOT	Chicago Board of Trade
CD	Certificate of Deposit
CDN	Canadian Dealing Network
CDS	Canadian Depository for Securities
CFTC	Commodity Futures Trading Commission
CGO	Central Gilts Office

CHAPS	Clearing House Automated Payment System
CHESS	Clearing House Electronic Sub Register System
CHIPS	Clearing House Interbank Payment System
CISCO	City Group for Smaller Companies
CLOB	Central Limit Order Book
CME	Chicago Mercantile Exchange
CMO	Central Moneymarkets Office
COMEX	Commodities Exchange in New York
COMPS	Contracted Out Money Purchase Scheme
CPA	Compulsory Purchase Annuity
DIE	Designated Investment Exchange
DTC	Depository Trust Company
DTI	Department of Trade and Industry
DVP	Delivery Versus Payment
EASDAQ	European Association of Securities Dealers Automated Quotation System
ECHO	Exchange Clearing House
ECSDA	European Central Securities Depository Association
ECU	European Currency Unit
EGM	Extraordinary General Meeting
EI	Expert Investor
EMU	Economic and Monetary Union
ESO	European Settlements Office
FAST	Fully Automated Securities Trading
FRA	Future Rate Agreement
FRN	Floating Rate Note
FSA 86	Financial Services Act (1986)
FSA	Financial Services Authority
FSAVC	Free-Standing Additional Voluntary Contribution
FTSE	Financial Times Stock Exchange Index
GDP	Gross Domestic Product
GNP	Gross National Product
GRY	Gross Redemption Yield

GSCC	Government Securities Clearing Corporation
IBRD	International Bank for Reconstruction and Development
ICAEW	Institute of Chartered Accountants in England and Wales
ICSA	Institute of Chartered Secretaries and Administrators
IFA	Independent Financial Adviser
IMRO	Investment Management Regulatory Organisation
IOSCO	International Organisation of Securities Commissions
IPC	Investment Protection Committee
IPE	International Petroleum Exchange
IPMA	International Primary Markets Association
ISA	Individual Savings Account
ISCC	International Securities Clearing Corporation
ISD	Intended Settlement Date/Investment Services Directive
ISIN	International Securities Identification Number
ISMA	International Securities Markets Association
ISSA	International Securities Services Association
JASDEC	Japan Securities Depository Centre
JATS	Jakarta Automated Trading System
JET	Johannesburg Electronic Trading
JSE	Johannesburg Stock Exchange
KSE	Korean Stock Exchange
LAN	Local Area Network
LCH	London Clearing House
LIBID	London Interbank Bid Rate
LIBOR	London Inter-Bank Offered Rate
LIFFE	London International Financial Futures and Options Exchange
LME	London Metal Exchange
LSE	London Stock Exchange

NAPF	National Association of Pension Funds
NASDAQ	National Association of Securities Dealers Automated Quotation System
NAV	Net Asset Value
NBV	Net Book Value
NCSD	National Central Securities Depository
NCIS	National Criminal Intelligence Service
NICs	National Insurance Contributions
NRY	Net Redemption Yield
NRE	Net Relevant Earnings
NSCC	National Securities Clearing Corporation
NYSE	New York Stock Exchange
OEICs	Open–Ended Investment Companies
OTC	Over The Counter
PHI	Permanent Health Insurance
PIBS	Permanent Interest Bearing Shares
PLC	Public Limited Company
PMI	Private Medical Insurance
POTOM	Panel on Take Overs and Mergers
PPP	Personal Pension Plan
RIE	Recognised Investment Exchange
RCH	Recognised Clearing House
RPB	Recognised Professional Body
SEATS	Stock Exchange Automated Trading System
SEAQ	Stock Exchange Automated Quotations System
SEHK	Stock Exchange of Hong Kong
SETS	Stock Exchange Electronic Trading System
SDRT	Stamp Duty Reserve Tax
SERPS	State Earnings Related Pension Scheme
SFA	Securities and Futures Authority
SHSE	Shanghai Stock Exchange
SIB	Securities and Investments Board
SIMA	Securities Industry Management Association

SIMEX	Singapore International Monetary Exchange
SPAN	Standard Portfolio ANalysis of risk
SRO	Self Regulating Organisation
SSCCR	Shanghai Securities Central Clearing and Registration Corporation
SSRC	Shenzhen Securities Registration Company
STRATE	Share Transactions Totally Electronic
SWIFT	Society for Worldwide Interbank Telecommunications
SWX	Swiss Stock Exchange
SZSE	Shenzhen Stock Exchange
TACT	Tel Aviv Continuous Trading
TARGET	Trans–European Automated Real–Time Gross Settlement System
TSCD	Taiwan Securities Central Depository
VAT	Value Added Tax

A

AAA Rating
The highest credit rating for a bond or company – the risk of default (or non-payment) is negligible.

A Day
The date – 29 April 1998 – when the Financial Services Act 1986 came into force.

A Shares
Ordinary shares that do not carry voting rights. They tend to be cheaper than ordinary shares and few still exist.

Abandonment
Allowing an option to expire worthless.

Acceptance
The act of accepting a rights issue or take over offer. See *Bankers Acceptance.*

Accrual Rate
The rate at which pension benefits build up each year with pensionable service in a defined benefit scheme. Accelerated accrual is an accrual rate of more than 1/60th of pensionable earnings for each year of service. Accrued benefits are the benefits from a pension scheme up to a particular point in time.

Accruals Accounting
Any expenses or income that have not been invoiced or paid when accounts are being drawn up are still included in the accounting figures.

Accrued Interest
In general, when traded, interest on bonds is separated from the underlying principal or price of the bond. When a bargain is transacted, the purchaser not only buys the underlying bond, but also the right to the next coupon payment, including the interest due for the period before the bond was purchased. In order to compensate the seller for this interest built up until the bargain date, the purchaser pays over an extra amount equivalent to the accrued interest, ie, the amount of interest due from the last coupon date to the time of purchase. Gilts and domestic bonds calculate using a 365–day year, whilst eurobonds usually assume a 360–day year. With the advent of the EURO, there is a move towards these conventions across Europe.

Accrued Rights Premium (ARP)
Premium paid by an employee to the state scheme for a pension member below state pensionable age to enable the state scheme, instead of the occupational scheme, to take over the provision to provide a GMP.

Accumulation Shares
Shares or units where net income is automatically reinvested and is reflected either in the value of the units or in additional units being allocated. The unit holder benefits from not having to pay an initial charge on the reinvested income.

ACD
See *Authorised Corporate Director*.

ACD's Box
See *Book/Box*.

ACT
Advance Corporation Tax.

Action for Damages
A provision under S.62 FSA 1986 for small investors to recover money lost. Only available if a breach of regulations has taken place. Large investors would instead have to sue for breach of contract.

Active Investment Management
This uses analysis to achieve above–average returns. The two techniques used are 1. stock selection, which uses fundamental analysis to identify undervalued stocks to buy and overvalued stocks to sell; and 2. market timing.

Active Market
A stock market where trading in securities is extremely active.

Activities Of Daily Living (ADL)
Criteria used for defining when a person may claim under certain insurance policies eg, long–term care. They include mobility, dressing, eating, continence, toileting and washing and bathing.

Actual/Actual
Calculation of accrued interest on a bond using the actual number of days of accrual and the actual number of days between interest payment dates – used in many government bond markets.

Actual Price
The price of any commodity which can be immediately sold or delivered.

Actual Settlement Date Accounting (ASDA)
Global custodians will give good cash value only on settlement of the securities trade itself.

Added Years
Extra pension benefits based on additional periods of pensionable service within a final salary pension scheme. Added years are often purchased through AVC schemes.

Additional Voluntary Contributions (AVCS)
Voluntary contributions made by a member of an occupational pension scheme over and above his or her normal contributions. They can buy either added years or be on a money purchase basis.

ADR
See *American Depositary Receipt*.

Advising
Giving advice to investors on specific investments with a view to it being acted upon.

Aftermarket
See *Secondary Market*.

After-hours trading
The facility whereby securities can be bought or sold at any time of the day after the relevant exchange is closed.

Agency Bargain
A trade that involves a client buying or selling stock through a broker dealer agent, with a broker dealer principal as the counterparty. Also known as an agent/principal bargain. Most agent/principal bargains involve a market maker as the principal.

Agency Cross Bargain
A type of bargain that occurs when one broker dealer agent buys and sells stock between one or more parties at the same price.

Agent/Agent Bargain
A trade that involves two London Stock Exchange member firms who are both acting in the capacity of broker dealer agents for their own clients. One agent's client is selling stock which the other agent's client is buying.

AGM
See *Annual General Meeting*.

AITC
Association of Investment Trust Companies.

Alleged
The description given to a transaction instruction which requires matching (eg, bargains, stock loans) but for which no matching instruction has been input. The unmatched instruction is said to be 'alleged' against the counterparty cited on the instruction.

Allocation
The process of moving the trade from the executing broker to the clearing broker. Also the division of a single market trade across two or more investors/funds.

Allotment Letter
A document issued to shareholder as proof of ownership of an underlying stock when a company has a rights issue or open offer entitling the shareholder to take up new shares. Some new issues commence trading in allotment letter form usually for the first six-week period before the stock becomes fully registered.

Alternative Investment Market (AIM)
The second tier or junior market established by the London Stock Exchange in 1995 to provide trading facilities in the shares of smaller companies.

Alternative Investments
Investment in physical assets such as antiques, jewellry, works of art etc.

American Depository Receipt (ADR)
Document giving the owner rights to UK shares which have been lodged in a US Depository. They are effectively bearer documents. They are issued by US banks to give American investors access to UK shares.

American Style Option
An option than can be exercised on any business day up to expiry.
See *European Style Option*.

Amsterdam Stock Exchange
The world's oldest exchange.

Amortisation
The gradual reduction over time of the principal of a bond or mortgage.

Annual General Meeting (AGM)
Meeting of shareholders which a company must call every year. Main purposes are to receive the accounts, vote on dividends and appoint directors.

Annual Management Charge
A charge usually in the order of 0.75 to 1.75% of the value of the fund levied for the management of a trust, PEP or other fund.

Annual Percentage Rate (APR)
The true cost of borrowing in terms of interest and fees, which must be shown on all advertisements for loans.

Annuity
A regular payment which may be level or subject to increases normally made until the death of the person receiving the annuity. Can be joint (2) names, in which case, payments continue till death of the second person.

Annuity Certain
Annuity which makes payments for a specified period of time regardless of whether the annuitant is alive or dead during that period.

APACS
Association for Payment Clearing Services, a group of major banks providing payment services.

APCIMS
Association of Private Client Investment Managers and Stockbrokers.

Appointed Representatives
Individuals or companies acting on behalf of an authorised person who take responsibility for everything done by the representative, who is exempt from obtaining his own authorisation.

Appropriate Personal Pension Scheme (APPS)
A personal pension scheme (or Free Standing AVC) which can be used for contracting out of the State Earning Related Pension Scheme (SERPS).

APR
See *Annual Percentage Rate*.

Arbitrage
The simultaneous sale (or purchase) of a financial instrument and the taking of an equal and opposite position in a similar instrument to give a profit, ie exploiting pricing anomalies across markets. True arbitrage should be risk free.

Arbitrageur
A trader who takes advantage of profitable opportunities arising from price anomalies.

Arm's Length
A transaction between financially unrelated companies.

Arranging
Having some positive role in an investment transaction.

Articles of Association
A document which sets out the rules by which shareholders and a company will be administered eg. voting rights. See *Memorandum of Association*.

Ask price
Price at which a market maker will sell stock. Also known as the offer price.

Asset Allocation
Any general allocation of funds across sectors or markets.

Assets
Something that has earning potential or value. See *Current Assets* and *Fixed Assets*.

Assignee
The person to whom an asset is transferred to.

Assignment
A transfer of ownership.

Assignor
The original beneficiary of an asset.

Association of British Insurers (ABI)
A trade body of insurance companies through which they can air their views collectively on matters of common concern.

Association of Lloyd's Members (ALM)
A non–official association which informs and represents Lloyd's of London members.

Assured
The person who has contracted with the life office, the original owner of the policy.

At Best Order
Any order to buy or sell at the prevailing prices in the market at the time the order is executed.

At–Call
See *Call Money*.

At-The-Money
An option whose strike price is equal to the current market price of the underlying instrument.

Auction
The method by which the Bank of England issues gilts. In an auction the investors specify the amount they wish to purchase and the price they are prepared to pay. Successful applicants then pay the price that they offered.

Auction Market Preferred Stock (AMPS)
Preference shares issued by a company which have a variable dividend and set at a market rate at regular periods by an auction between investors.

Audit
The independent verification of financial statements of a company by an independent firm of accountants.

Audit Trail
A historical record of all price quotations and transactions. Checks can be made to ensure that the buying and selling of securities has been carried out in an accurate manner.

Authentication
The technical process of ensuring that all messages and files sent across a communications network are from the purported source and have not been modified in transit.

Authorisation
Status required by the Financial Services Act 1986 for any firm that wants to conduct investment business. It is achieved by direct application to FSA or by becoming a member of an SRO.

Authorised Corporate Director (ACD)
A corporate body and an authorised person given powers and duties under FSA regulations to operate an OEIC.

Authorised Investments
Trustees may take on responsibility for investments under the Trustee Investments Act 1961.

Authorised Person
A Firm authorised by the Financial Services Authority, an SRO or RPB to conduct investment business in the UK.

Authorised Unit Trust
A unit trust scheme authorised by FSA. A UK unit trust must be authorised before it can be offered to the general public in the UK.

AUTIF
Association of Unit Trusts and Investment Funds. The trade association for the collective investment industry.

Automated Pit Trading (APT) System
The automated trading system used by LIFFE, usually for after hours trading.

Automatic Accrual
An agreement under which a deceased partner's share passes automatically to the surviving partners. The partners agree to insure their lives for their shares in the value of the business.

AVCs
See *Additional Voluntary Contributions*.

B

Back Office
The settlement, processing and accounting departments of a bank or broking firm. Now more usually referred to as 'operations'.

Back–to–Back Loans
A method of hedging foreign exchange risk where, for example, a fund's base currency is sterling and the investments are based on a foreign currency.

Back–to–Back Plan
A combination of a life assurance policy and an annuity.

Backwardation
A situation where the offer price of one market maker is lower than the bid price of others.

BACS
Bank Automated Clearing System. A debit and credit system used to make direct transfers to/from clients' accounts.

Bad Delivery
The situation in which a company registrar rejects a request to transfer shares or stock ownership so the transfer is not registered.

Balance Certificate
Certificate issued where the number of shares being sold is less than the number of shares shown on the certificate.

Balance Sheet
A financial statement showing, at a point in time, the assets and liabilities of a company and how the assets have been financed by shareholders.

Balance of Payments
The accounts of a country's trade with other countries. If imports are higher there is a deficit and if exports are higher there is a surplus.

Ballot
A method used to allocate shares in a new issue, when there are more applications than available shares.

Bancassurance
The amalgamation of assurance and banking business within a financial environment ie: bank or building society.

Bank – Commercial
Organisation that is licensed to take deposits and can make loans.

Bank – Merchant
Organisation that specialises in advising on takeovers and corporate finance activities.

Bank of England
The UK's central bank which undertakes overall monetary policy and determines interest rates.

Bank of England Register
Gilts purchased through a stockbroker are normally registered on the Bank of England Register and interest is payable subject to deduction of tax.

Bankers Acceptance
A bill of exchange that has been endorsed and accepted payable by a bank for guarantee of payment of the face value of the bill at maturity date.

Barber v Gre (1990)
The case before the European Court which ruled that from 17 May 1990, men and women in occupational pension schemes have rights to the same retirement age and not to be discriminated against generally. The date from which this was to be effected was confirmed in the Maastricht Protocol 1993.

Bargain
A Stock Exchange or unit trust buy/sell transaction.

Base Currency
The foreign exchange deal currency against which another currency is measured.

Base Rate
The rate of interest used as a basis by UK banks to make loans to their customers.

Basic Pension
State pension payable to all those with an adequate NIC payments record.

Basis Point (bp)
A measure which is mainly used in the statement of interest rates. One hundredth of 1% – 25 basis points is equal to 0.25%.

Basis Risk
The risk that the price of a derivative instrument will vary from that of the underlying commodity.

Basis Swap
An interest rate swap where the interest payments that are exchanged between each party are based on different indexes.

BBA
British Bankers' Association.

Bear
A person who sells shares he or she does not hold in the hope of buying them back at a lower price. The term describes someone who thinks a price will fall.

Bear Call Spread
The buying and selling of two calls that have the same expiry date where the option bought is at a higher exercise price than the one sold.

Bear Market
A market in which prices are falling.

Bear Put Spread
The buying and selling of two puts that have the same expiry date where the option bought is at a higher exercise price than the one sold.

Bearer Document
Documents which state on them that the person in physical possession (the bearer) is the owner.

Bearer Securities
Securities for which there is no register of beneficial ownership. For certificated bearer securities, the certificate itself is proof of ownership. Dividends (for shares) and interest (bonds) are collected by clipping the coupons from the certificate and sending them to the paying agent.

Bearer Shares
Shares which transfer by hand without the need for registration of the change of ownership.

Bed and Breakfasting
Procedure whereby securities were sold on one day and re–purchased on the following day. The reason being to establish the gain or loss on disposal for Capital Gains Tax purposes. Will effectively not be allowed from April 1999 when any repurchase within 30 days of a sale will be ignored for CGT purposes.

Bed and PEPing
Selling shares or units held in the investor's own name to provide the cash subscription for a PEP. Usually the purchase of shares or units for the PEP is made at the same time for simultaneous settlement.

Benchmark Bond
Used as a comparison with which the attractiveness or worth of other bonds might be judged.

Beneficial Owner
The underlying owner of a security who has paid for the stock and is entitled to the benefits of ownership.

Benefit Distribution
Corporate actions in which cash and/or stock distributions are made by companies to their shareholders. Benefits are usually distributed in proportion to the investor's holding. Examples include: dividends and scrip dividends, rights issues and capitalisations (bonus issues). See *Corporate Action*.

Best Advice
Duty on financial advisers to recommend products that are the most suitable for the client.

Best Execution
Dealing for a client at the best available price for the size and kind of transaction concerned.

Beta
A measure of how much a stock will move in relation to an index. It is a measure of its volatility and therefore its risk.

Better Than Best
Obligation on Independent Financial Advisors (IFAs) when they recommend the product of a connected person.

Bid
The rate at which the market or a particular trader is willing to buy.

Bid/Offer Spread
The standard differential between the price of buying and selling securities. It is usually quoted as a monetary amount for shares, a percentage term for unit trusts.

Bid Basis
A fund is said to be on a bid basis if it is priced on the basis of the minimum bid price required by regulations laid down by the Financial Services Authority.

Bid Price
The price at which units are sold back to the managers by investors. The difference between the bid and offer prices is know as the bid and offer spread – generally about 6% on an equity unit trust.

Also the price at which a market maker will buy a share from an investor. See *Ask Price, Middle Price*.

Big Bang
The change in the rules of the Stock Exchange which occurred on 27th October 1986, so called because the abolition of fixed commissions precipitated a complete alteration in the structure of the stock market.

Bilateral Payment
A payment type, indicating arrangements where a payment bank settles its payment obligations on a net basis with each of its counterparty banks separately.

Bill of Exchange
An unconditional order in writing, addressed by one person to another, signed by the person giving it, requiring the person to whom it is addressed to pay on demand or at a fixed period in the future, a sum of money, to the order of a specified person, or to bearer.

Black Monday
On Monday 19 October 1997, the world stock market prices crashed.

Black Scholes
A theoretical option pricing model widely used in the market. Named after Fischer Black and Myron Scholes.

Blue Chip
Originally an American expression, to denote the shares of companies which are well established, usually large and highly regarded.

Board Lot
A standard dealing quantity of shares. Also called a round lot. Dealing is normally in multiples of the board lot. cf Odd Lot.

Bobl
German government security issued with a 5 year maturity (Bundesobligationen).

Bona Fide
In good faith, without fraud or deceit.

Bond
An alternative name for fixed interest securities. Normally a single premium life assurance policy, either guaranteed or unit–linked. Normally a non–qualifying policy.

Bond Borrowing
Authorised organisations borrow bonds from institutional investors or other organisations with long positions in exchange for a fee. See *Bond Lending*.

Bond House
A securities firm that creates, distributes and markets bonds.

Bond Lending
Authorised organisations and institutional investors make their long positions available to organisations who have short positions or short–term settlement fails. The lender receives a fee for this service See *Bond Borrowing*.

Bonus
Profit allocated to a with profits policy. Once allocated cannot be withdrawn.

Bonus Issue
A free issue of shares to a company's existing shareholders. No money changes hands and the share price falls pro rata. It is a cosmetic exercise to make the shares more marketable. Also known as a capitalisation or scrip issue.

Book/Box
The stock of units owned by managers acting as principals. Incoming unit holders buy their units from managers. If the managers act only as agents for the trustee in the issue of units, then units are transferred directly into the unit holder's name (i.e. not from the managers) and all the dealings with the fund by investors are effected at maximum spread.

Book Cost
The original cost of an investment generally used to compare against the current market value.

Book Entry
The term to describe the electronic recording of an asset which is either in an immobilised or dematerialised form.

Book Entry Transfer
A method whereby the transfer of ownership of securities is effected electronically by debits and credits to accounts without the need for the movement of physical certificates or documents.

Books Closed Day
Last date for registration of shares or bonds for the payment of the next dividend or interest payment, or for processing a Corporate Action.

Book Runner
An organisation responsible for a bond from its initial launch through to issue and maintaining a secondary market.

Book Transfer
A type of payment where the clearing house debits the participants cash account and credits the funds internally to the beneficiary's participant cash account. See *Wire Transfer*.

Bottom up management
A method of active portfolio management where securities are selected on their own merits without consideration of the asset class or security sector.

Box
Name given to the system through which unit trust managers store units that have been redeemed by unit holders for subsequent onward sale.

Bretton Woods
The US venue of a conference in 1944 which established a system of fixed exchange rates, the International Monetary Fund and the World Bank.

Bridge
An electronic link between CEDEL and Euroclear, the two Eurobond clearing houses.

Bridging Pension
A scheme may provide a temporary extra pension equal to state benefits between scheme retirement age and state retirement age.

British Government Stocks
See *Gilts*.

British Standards Institution (BSI)
The UK national standards body which is a member of ISO. Recognises the Technical Standards Committee as the focal point for input to the UK and ISO standards setting process on behalf of practitioners in the UK Securities Industry.

Broken Date
A value date outside the normal run of money market value dates (1,2,3,6,12 months).

Broker
Bank or other institution which acts as an intermediary, bringing together buyers and sellers or borrowers and lenders.

Broker/Dealer
Any member firm of the Stock Exchange except the specialists which are Gilt Edged Market Makers (GEMMs) and Inter–dealer Brokers (IDBs).

Broker Dealer Agent
A member firm of the London Stock Exchange who is authorised by the Exchange to trade on behalf of clients. Sometimes called an 'agent'.

Broker Dealer Principal
A member firm of the London Stock Exchange who is authorised by the Exchange to trade as a wholesaler, buying and selling stock on his own behalf. A market maker is a specific type of broker dealer principal.

Brokerage
The commission charged by a broker.

Broking
The activity of representing a client as agent and charging commission for doing so.

BSI
See *British Standards Institution*.

BTAN
French government bond issued with a maturity of either 2 or 5 years.

Bull
Someone who expects a share/unit price will rise.

Bull Call Spread
The buying and selling of two calls with the same expiry date where the option bought is at a lower price than the one sold.

Bull Market
A market in which prices are rising.

Bull Put Spread
The buying and selling of two puts with the same expiry date where the option bought is at a lower price than the one sold.

Bulldog Bond
A bond denominated in sterling, issued on behalf of a non–resident borrower and listed on the London Stock Exchange.

Bullet Bond
A bond for which there is one single repayment on maturity by the borrower with no amortisation clauses.

Bund
German government bond issued with maturity between 8 or 30 years (Bundesanleihen).

Business Day
Any day other than a Saturday, Sunday, Christmas Day, Good Friday or a bank holiday under the Banking and Financial Dealings Act 1971.

Business Expansion Scheme (BES)
An investment scheme that ended 31 December 1993 for new investment. Tax relief was available on subscriptions to shares in qualifying companies. Proceeds were tax-free after five years.

Buy and Sell Agreement
An agreement between partners or shareholder directors for a deceased person's estate to sell their share of the business/company and the survivors to buy it.

Buyer's Guide
Document that must be provided to all prospective purchasers of long term insurance products which explains the difference between an independent financial adviser and a company representative and identifies the status of the person supplying the document.

Buying-in
A mechanism which, in the case of non-delivery of securities by a seller, gives a buyer the chance to receive the securities by buying them from another counterparty. The original deal is subsequently closed out.

C

CAC 40
Index of the Paris Stock Exchange comprising the top 40 listed shares.

CBOE
Chicago Board Options Exchange.

CBOT
Chicago Board of Trade.

CME
Chicago Mercantile Exchange.

Cable
Dealers' word for the USD/GBP exchange rate.

Calendar Spread
Options trading strategy where one option is bought and another sold, the two contracts have the same exercise prices but different expiry dates.

Call
The early redemption of bonds at the bond issuer's option.

Call Money
A loan or deposit that has no fixed maturity date.

Call Option
A call option bestows the right to buy an underlying asset at a given price. The short seller (also known as the writer) has an obligation to sell shares to the holder, if the option is exercised.

Call Payments
Payments made by allotment letter holders when taking up a share offer, eg, in a rights issue or privatisation. Call payments must be made by the acceptance date specified in the allotment letter.

Callable Bond
A bond with the issuer's right to redeem the principal amount early.

Cancellation Price
This is the lowest price at which the Authorised Corporate Directors (ACDs) may repurchase shares and the price which an ACD receives for a share when he cancels shares off his book/box. Also applies to Unit Trust Managers.

Cancellation Rights
Under the Financial Services (Non–Life Cancellation) Rules 1997, there are certain circumstances under which an investor has the right to cancel a purchase of shares, but cancellation rights only apply if the investment was made through an independent financial adviser, or after receiving advice from a company representative of the fund manager. They are not available for execution–only transactions or where terms of business with the IFA exclude cancellation rights.

Cancellation Rules
The rules which allow purchasers of certain products a period of time (cooling off period) during which they can change their minds and cancel the agreement.

Cap
An option which fixes a maximum interest rate payable for a series of interest periods. Also a line of credit agreed between a CREST or CGO participant and their Settlement Bank.

Capital Account (Balance Of Payments)
Surplus or deficit between the UK and overseas on the movement of both short term and long term flows of investment money.

Capital Adequacy
Requirement for firms conducting investment business to have sufficient funds.

Capital Adequacy Directive (CAD)
European Union Directive implemented in the UK in January 1996. It establishes minimum funding requirements for all Intended Settlement Date (ISD) businesses.

Capital Bonds (National Savings)
National Savings product designed for lump sum investments. Return is maximised if held for five years and is liable to income tax.

Capital Employed
The total of fixed assets plus current assets less current liabilities. It also means the shareholders' funds plus borrowing.

Capital Gains Tax (CGT)
Capital gains tax is payable by the individual taxpayer at rate equivalent to the taxpayer's highest rate of income tax on gains (over £7,100 for 1999/00) arising from the sale of securities or other chargeable assets. Most trusts will be exempt on the first £3,550 of gains.

Capital Markets
The means by which large amounts of money (capital) are raised by companies, governments and other organisations for long term use and the subsequent trade of the instruments issued in recognition of such capital. New money is raised in the *Primary* market by issuing shares or bonds to investors who can then trade them on the relevant *Secondary* market.

Capital Protected Annuity
Annuity where the total payments will not be less than the cost of the annuity.

Capital Repayment
A corporate action in which the company partly repays the capital in issue by paying the holders a proportion of the paid–up capital of the security.

Capital Asset Pricing Model (CAPM)
Economic theory describing the relationship between security returns and risk.

Capitalisation
The value of a company in terms of issued share capital. It is the number of shares x price quotation.

Capitalisation Issue
A corporate action (also known as a bonus issue) in which a company issues fully paid shares to existing shareholders as a result of a rearrangement of a company's capital structure. The issue does not result in any new funds for the company.

Carry
The cost of holding an inventory or portfolio of securities after deducting the funding costs from the interest received.

Cash flow statement
Financial statement showing the major cash flows of a company for a year.

Cash Market
The market in an underlying instrument, on which a derivative instrument is based.

Cash Memorandum Account (CMA)
The record of the running total of each member's payment obligations kept by CREST throughout the day.

CB
Convertible Bond. See *Convertible*.

CCJ
County Court Judgment.

CCSS
See *CREST Courier and Sorting Service*.

CCT
Italian government FRN issued with maturities of 5,7 and 10 years

Cedel Bank
Founded in September 1970 by participants in the Eurobond market, Cedel provides clearing, settlement and custody for a wide range of internationally traded Eurobonds, domestic bonds and equities. Cedel is one of two International Central Securities Depositories; the other being Euroclear.

Central
The default payment type for UK and Irish registered securities, indicating that payment obligations between payment banks are settled on a multilaterally–netted basis, eg, each bank makes or receives a single payment in settlement of all that day's payment business in CREST.

Central Bank
The bank that provides financial and banking services to the government of a country and its commercial banking system and which implements the government's monetary policy.

Central Gilts Office (CGO)
Book entry transfer system for gilts run by the Bank of England.

Central Moneymarkets Office (CMO)
The central clearing house for money market securities.

Central Securities Depository (CSD)
The principal function of a CSD is to immobilise or dematerialise securities, assuring that the bulk of securities transactions are processed in book–entry form. CSDs may also have the capability for trade clearance, safe custody and settlement/post settlement processing of securities and information. (Refer also to International CSDs, National CSDs, Euroclear and Cedel.)

Certificate
A document issued by the issuer of a security stating either that a named person is the registered owner or that the bearer is the owner.

Certificate of Deposit
A negotiable instrument issued by a bank in return for a fixed deposit of up to five years

Certificated Holdings
Holdings of securities which are evidenced by paper certificates instead of an entry in a dematerialised account.

Certificated Securities
Securities represented in the form of a paper certificates.

Certification
The process of authorising a stock transfer form to be deposited and registered without the cover of a share certificate.

CFTC
The Commodity Futures Trading Commission (United States).

CGO
See *Central Gilts Office*.

CHAPS
See *Clearing House Automated Payment System*.

Charts, chartism
An example of technical analysis that involves plotting graphs and charts to identify share price movement. This knowledge can aid decisions as to when to buy and sell.

Children's Bonus Bonds
National Savings product which enables parents to save money for children in a tax efficient way.

Chinese Walls
Artificial barriers to the flow of information set up in large firms to prevent the movement of sensitive information between departments.

CHIPS
See *Clearing House Interbank Payments System*.

Churning
Excessive trading which permits the broker to derive a profit from commissions, while disregarding the best interests of the customer.

Circles
A CREST process which attempts to settle a series of transactions that are mutually dependent on each other's settlement.

Circuit breaker
An arrangement which, at times of high price volatility, halts trading on a stock exchange for a short period.

CISCO
City Group for Smaller Companies.

City Code
Principles and rules written by Panel on Takeovers and Mergers to regulate conduct during a takeover.

City Panel
Panel on Takeovers and Mergers: A non–statutory body which enforces the Takeover Code and Substantial Acquisition Rules.

Claims Processing Unit (CPU)
The part of CREST which identifies transactions settling through the system where parties entitled to receive a benefit distribution (e.g a dividend) failed to appear on the legal register in time to receive the benefit directly.

Class
All calls and puts, of the same type, on one underlying instrument.

Claw Back
The recovery by the Inland Revenue of Life Assurance Premium Relief (LAPR) given under a life assurance policy.

Clean Payment
A payment of cash for which there is no directly associated countervalue.

Clean Price
The price of a bond before any adjustment has been made. See *Dirty Price*.

Clearing
The centralised process whereby transacted business is recorded and positions are maintained.

Clearing House
An organisation which guarantees the performance and settlement of futures and options contracts, eg. the London Clearing House in London or the Options Clearing Corporation in Chicago.

Clearing House Automated Payment System (CHAPS)
System in the UK for making cash payments in sterling. The recipient receives same day funds.

Clearing House Interbank Payments System (CHIPS)
Electronic means of settling banking payments in New York.

Clearing Member
A member of an exchange who has met the criteria, and undertakes to settle the derivatives business which is registered in its name at the clearing organisation.

Clearing System
A system for transferring bonds and cash between buyers and sellers. Transfers of bonds are usually made by book entry transfer.

Client Agreement Letter
A legal agreement between client and broker, setting out terms and conditions for the broking arrangement.

Client Money
Money belonging to clients which an investment business is holding. It could either be free money or settlement money and in either case it must be kept in a bank account separate from the firm's own money.

Close Company
A company where five or fewer people and their associates (eg families) control over 50% of the votes.

Closed ended Scheme
A collective investment scheme which has a fixed capital, or a share capital which can be changed only after the completion of certain formalities.

Closing
The procedure whereby obligations under an existing position in a derivative are cancelled by undertaking a transaction which is the reverse of the original one.

Closing the books
A Registrar closing his register for the payment of a dividend etc.

Closing Date
The last date by which a new issue should be taken up and paid for.

Closing Trade
A trade to reduce an investor's position. A closing buy reduces a short position and a closing sale reduces a long position.

CMA
See *Cash Memorandum Account*.

CME
Chicago Mercantile Exchange.

CMO
See *Central Moneymarkets Office*.

Cold Call
See *Unsolicited Call*.

Collar
In an options market, the simultaneous purchase of a 'cap' and then sale of a 'floor' to protect an investor against fluctuations in interest rates.

Collateral
A borrower will pledge collateral (securities, property etc) in order to demonstrate their ability to meet their obligations to repay monies loaned.

Collective Investment Schemes
A generic term encompassing authorised unit trusts, common investment funds, OEICs and investment trusts.

Collective Investment Schemes Regulations
Industry name for The Financial Services (Regulated Schemes) Regulations 1991 published by FSA.

Co–Manager
A bank or bond house that assists a lead manager in assessing and distributing new bond issues. A co–manager will receive a larger allotment of bonds than the underwriters to an issue.

Combination
An options trade which involves both calls and puts on the same underlying asset.

Commercial Bank
A bank specialising in the provision of retail banking services to the corporate and individual banking sectors.

Commercial Paper (CP)
A short–term debt instrument issued by a company. Often issued as part of a longer term programme. It is an example of a money market instrument.

Commission
A fee paid to an agent for services rendered, and often expressed as a percentage of the value of the deal.

Commodity
Any item that can be bought and sold. Taken to refer to Exchange–traded items including sugar, wheat, soya beans, coffee and tin.

Commodity Futures
Contracts to supply quantities of the underlying commodity at a future date.

Common Stock
See *Equity shares*.

Companies Act 1989
An Act of Parliament which made several changes and amendments to the Companies Act 1985, the Financial Services Act 1986 and the Company Securities (Insider Dealing) Act 1985 etc.

Company
A business entity, ownership of which is divided into units called shares, which are owned by persons called shareholders who have limited liability. The business is managed by persons called directors.

Company Representative
Name given to employee of a financial services provider who is only allowed to recommend that company's products.

Complaints Bureau
An FSA service provided for customers who have made a written complaint to a member firm and are still dissatisfied.

Complaints Commissioner
Monitors the activities of the SFA Complaints Bureau.

Complaints Procedure
Any SRO procedure whereby customer complaints about late payments and other inefficiencies by brokers can be made. To start with, the complaint would be made to a firm, and if the customer is still not happy to the SRO itself.

Compliance Officer
Person appointed within an authorised firm to be responsible for ensuring compliance with the rules.

Compound Interest
Interest calculated each period on the amount outstanding at the beginning of that period including any interest previously earned.

Compulsory Purchase Annuity (CPA)
An annuity that has to be bought at retirement for a member of an occupational pension scheme retiring from service.

Concert Party
Investors buying securities in agreement between themselves to suit some wider purpose (eg, to evade the disclosure rules of the Takeover Panel).

Conciliation Service
A confidential service provided by SFA for customers of brokers whose complaints have not been satisfied by the member firm or the SFA Complaints Bureau.

Conduct of Business Rules
Rules required by the Financial Services Act 1986 to dictate how firms conduct their business. They deal mainly with the relationship between firm and client.

Confirm
An agreement for each individual Over the Counter (OTC) transaction which has specific terms.

Confirmation
An acknowledgement of a securities transaction between two counterparties.

Confirmation Note
Confirmation of the details of a transaction. Other descriptions would include Advice Note or Acknowledgment.

Conflicts of Interest
Circumstances that arise where a firm has an investment which could encourage it not to treat its clients favourably. The more areas in which a firm is involved the greater the number of potential conflicts.

Consideration
The value of a contract for buying or selling financial instruments before commission and charges have been applied.

Consolidation
A corporate action in which a company proportionally increases the nominal value of each share whilst decreasing the number of shares in issue. A consolidation is effectively the opposite of a subdivision.

Consumer Price Index
A measurement of retail price inflation.

Contango
Where the spot price is lower than longer term prices. See *Backwardation*.

Contingent Liability Transaction
A derivatives transaction where a customer may be liable to make further payments in the future, depending on the movement of the price.

Continuation Option
Option offered by an insurance company for a pension scheme member leaving a scheme to take out a life assurance policy (or PHI or PMI policy) without evidence of health.

Continuing Obligations
Rules for listed companies, particularly on disclosure of information on an ongoing basis – detailed in the Yellow Book.

Contract
The standard trading unit for a future or an option, also known as a 'lot'. The contract size for UK equity options is 1000 underlying shares.

Contract for differences
Contract designed to make a profit or avoid a loss by reference to movements in the price of an item. The underlying item cannot change hands.

Contract Note
A document sent to the investor on a purchase or sale being made, detailing the price at which the shares were bought, sold or redeemed together with other charges, any conditions of sale and statutory notes.

Contracted Out Money Purchase Scheme (COMPS)
A money purchase scheme which is contracted out of SERPS by providing protected rights.

Contracted Out Rebate
The amount by which employers' and employees' NICs are reduced for employees who are contracted out through an occupational scheme.

Contractual Capacity
The legal ability to make a contract.

Contractual Income Collection
The policy by which global custodians agree to credit income on or after a pre-determined number of days after the official pay-date irrespective of the actual date of receipt.

Contractual Settlement Date Accounting (CSDA)
Global custodians will, in certain conditions and in pre-determined countries, give clients good cash value for securities trades irrespective (subject to certain conditions) of the settlement of the securities themselves.cf Actual Settlement Date Accounting.

Controlling Director
A director who controls or owns 20% or more of the ordinary shares of his or her employing company. The shares of associates (eg. family members) are taken into account. Special restrictions apply to such directors who are members of occupational pension schemes.

Conversion
A type of corporate action involving, for example, the transformation of a debt security into shares or other forms of debt.

Conversion Factor
Income shares and accumulation shares are linked by a conversion factor so from day to day the two types of share will always move in line. Each time the income units are quoted xd the conversion factor is adjusted, so there will be a proportionate difference between the two types of share. The conversion factor tells you that each accumulation unit is the equivalent of that number of income shares. The factor is calculated to 5 significant figures.

Conversion Period
The period during which a bondholder may convert the bond into shares.

Conversion Premium
A measure of the effective cost of acquiring the underlying shares by either converting the bond or buying the shares in the market.

Conversion Price
The price, specified in the issue prospectus, at which the nominal amount of the bond may be converted into the shares.

Conversion Rate
The number of shares that result from the conversion of one bond.

Convertible
A convertible is a debt instrument, paying a fixed coupon, which offers the holder the right (but not the obligation) to covert into the underlying shares of a company (usually, but not always, the issuing company).

Convertible Bond
A bond that can be converted at the choice of the bondholder into the shares of the issuer. The bondholder receives redemption proceeds on maturity of a bond which has not been converted.

Convertible Loan Stock
A fixed interest loan stock where the investor has the right to convert it or part of it into an agreed number of shares at a fixed time.

Convertible Term Assurance
Type of term assurance which carries an option to convert to whole life or endowment.

Convertible Unsecured Loan Stock (CULS)
A convertible bond which is not backed by any specific asset.

Conveyancing
The legal transfer of ownership of land or property, normally carried out by a solicitor or licensed conveyancer.

Cooling-Off Period
The period in which investors have the chance to change their mind and withdraw from a life assurance policy or some other financial service – 14 days.

CORES
Computer dealing system of the Tokyo Stock Exchange.

Corporate Action
A term given to an action taken by a company which distributes cash, stock or a combination to shareholders or stock holders, usually in proportion to the investor's holding (ie, benefit distribution) or which changes the nature or description of a company's stock (ie, stock event). Corporate actions include dividends, rights issues, redemptions, consolidations, placings, etc. See also CA type.

Corporate Finance
General title which covers activities such as raising cash through new issues of securities and merger/acquisitions.

Corporate Investor
A company that holds shares in another company solely for its own benefit.

Corporation Tax
Taxation paid by companies on its assessable profits.

Correlation
The extent to which two sets of data move in line with each other.

Correspondent
A financial organisation that regularly performs services for another in a place or market to which the other does not have direct access. Banks will, for example, use correspondent banks to hold their foreign currency accounts.

Cost Of Carry
The cost of financing a position. See *Position*.

Counterparty
One of the parties to a transaction – either the buyer or the seller.

Countervalue
The cash amount to be received in return for a specified delivery of securities.

Coupon
The percentage rate of interest payable on a bond. The figure shown is always the pre–tax (gross) rate.

Coupon Clipping
The process by which coupons are detached from the certificates prior to collection of the interest payment.

Coupon Payment Period
The time that has elapsed between two consecutive interest payments on a bond.

Covariance
Measure of the co–movement between two variables (eg. security prices). It is particularly important in modern portfolio theory which examines the relationships of individual shares within a portfolio of shares (or other securities)

Covered Sale (Write)
The situation where an option writer has existing holdings to cover a position, eg where the writer of a call owns the underlying stock or where the writer of a put is either short of stock or has sufficient cash (or near cash) to cover an assignment.

CPU
See *Claims Processing Unit*.

Credit Control
The regulation of credit of banks and other financial institutions in the pursuit of monetary policy.

Credit Creation
Ability of private sector banks to expand the money supply by creating credit.

Credit Derivatives
These are contracts designed to transfer the credit risk on loans or other assets from one party to another. There are four main types of contract: credit default swaps, total return swaps, credit–linked notes and credit spread options.

Credit Rating
For example, AAA issued by companies such as Standard & Poors, and Moodys to rate the level of security of a bond or note issue.

Credit Risk
The risk that a counterparty will be unable to perform his side of an agreed contract.

Creditor
Person to whom money is owed.

CREST
The book–entry transfer system for UK and Irish registered equities and corporate stocks.

CREST Courier and Sorting Service
The organisation responsible for the controlled transportation of documents, supporting the administration for settling deliveries in certificated securities.

CREST Member
A person or organisation participating in CREST (typically a broker, institutional investor, custodian, market maker, money broker, or inter–dealer broker) who holds stock in accounts with the system and whose name is on the register as the owner of securities.

CREST Member Accounts
One or more separate designations (identities) set up by a CREST member for holding stock. The member account facility enables members to segregate holdings of different kinds, eg, individual client holdings, although the member's name is on the register for each member account, designated by that code.

CREST Operator
The organisation at the centre of CREST responsible for system security, for settlement and for maintaining records of its members' stock holdings and reconciling them with the records of legal title held by company registrars. It also provides various functions to facilitate settlement of transactions between its members.

CREST Participant
A person or organisation that has a formal relationship with CREST, eg, members, registrars, receiving agents, payment banks, regulators, the Inland Revenue, and information providers.

CRESTCo
Organisation which owns CREST.

Criminal Justice Act 1993
Act which contains the legislation on Insider Dealing and Money Laundering.

Critical Illness Policy
A policy which pays out on the diagnosis of a critical illness as defined by the policy. Where the policy is part of an endowment or whole-life plan, the payment may be made on earlier maturity or death.

Cross Border Custody
Cross border custody occurs where the securities are actually held in custody in a country different from the domicile of the owner of the securities. It is not necessarily a result of cross border trading or settlement.

Cross Border Settlement
Cross border settlement occurs where the settlement takes place in a country different from the domicile of one or both trading parties.

Cross Border Trade
A cross border trade occurs where the trading parties are in different countries.

Cross Currency Interest Rate Swap
An interest rate swap where the interest payments are in two different currencies and the exchange rate, for the final settlement, is agreed at the outset of the transaction.

Cross Default
The right of a lender to accelerate the repayment of a debt if the borrower defaults on the repayment of another debt.

Cross Rate
An exchange rate between two currencies that does not involve a standard reference currency such as the USD.

CULS
A bond that can be converted into shares of the issuing company on terms specified at the time of issue. Called a convertible bond or Convertible Unsecured Loan Stock.

Cum
Latin for "with". Refers to the right to receive a benefit or entitlement on securities that have been purchased.

Cum Distribution
Unit trusts are assumed to be cum distribution (i.e. the buyer is entitled to the next income distribution and the seller is not) unless they are expressly stated to be ex–distribution.

Cum Dividend – Purchase/Sale
Shares purchased will be entitled to the next dividend payment. Shares sold will not be entitled to the next dividend payment.

Cum Rights Price
Share price before a rights issue takes place.

Cum Scrip Price
Share price before a scrip issue takes place.

Cum Period
During a benefit distribution, the period before ex date when a buyer of stock is normally contractually entitled to a benefit, whether or not he is on the register as at record date.

Cumulative Preference Share
If a company fails to pay a preference dividend the entitlement to the dividend accumulates and the arrears of the preference dividend must be paid before any ordinary dividend.

Currency Futures
Contracts calling for delivery of a specific amount of a foreign currency at a specified future date in return for a given amount of, say, US Dollars.

Currency Swap
It is an agreement to exchange interest–related payments in the same currency from fixed rate into floating rate (or vice versa) or from one type of floating rate to another. Principal amounts are also swapped.

Current Account (Balance Of Payments)
A statement of imports and exports of visibles and invisibles.

Current Assets
The assets of a company which are in cash or easily sold to raise cash, for example, bank balances, stocks, inventories and accounts receivable.

Current Liabilities
The obligations of a company that are payable within 12 months of the balance sheet date, for example, bank overdrafts, short–term loans and accounts payable.

Current Maturity
The remaining life of a bond from today to the redemption date.

Current Yield
A measure of the annual income on a bond as a percentage of the price of the bond.

Custodian
An institution holding stock on behalf of clients.

Customer – non-private
A customer who is assumed to understand the workings of the investment world and therefore receives little protection from the Conduct of Business Rules.

Customer – private
A customer who is assumed to be financially unsophisticated and therefore receives more protection from the Conduct of Business Rules.

Customer Agreement
A written contract detailing the basis on which services are to be provided to the customer by the firm.

Customer Borrowing
Funds lent to private customers by member firms.

Customer Order Priority
SFA Rule requiring a firm to deal with a customer and their own account orders fairly and in due turn.

Cycle
The expiry dates applicable to a class of options. There are three cycles in London: Jan/Apr/Jul/Oct; Feb/May/Aug/Nov; Mar/Jun/Sep/Dec.

D

Daily Official List (DOL)
A daily publication of the London Stock Exchange which lists the trading prices of securities traded in the main market.

Data Exchange Manual (DEX)
The document that gives full details of CREST messages and interface specifications for the file transfer interface.

Dated Stock
An interest bearing security that has a stated date for redemption or repayment.

DAX
Index of the German Stock Exchange.

Daylight Exposure
The deliverer of securities or payer of countervalue is exposed to the risk that the counterparty may default on his obligations at some stage during that business day.

Dealing
Entering into transactions in investments either for others or on one's own account.

Debenture
A fixed interest security issued in return for long-term loans; these are usually dated to be redeemed 10–40 years hence. Interest on this form of loan has to be paid by a company whether it makes a profit or not.

Debt/Equity Ratio
A measurement of gearing defined as:

$$\frac{\text{Borrowings + Preference shares}}{\text{Ordinary shareholders funds}} \times 100\%$$

For example, the debt equity ratio for XYZ Ltd is:

$$\frac{\text{(loan stock) + (preference shares)}}{\text{(shareholders funds) - (preference shares)}} \times 100\%$$

$$\frac{\$60m + \$10m}{\$120m - \$10m} \times 100\%$$

$$= 63.6\%$$

Debt Securities
Securities created by the issuer as evidence of a loan made to it, such as bonds, certificates of deposit (CDs), commercial paper.

Decreasing Term Assurance
Type of term assurance where the amount of cover decreases over the life of the policy. Often used in conjunction with repayment mortgages.

Deep Discount Bond

Stock issued at a low price compared with par value and redemption price. The rate of interest and the running yield are low, indeed may be zero, with most or all of the benefit to the investor coming from the capital gain between the issue and redemption prices. The benefit of deep discount bonds to the issuing company is the low interest commitment; to the high rate taxpayer they provide (relatively low tax) capital gain instead of (more highly taxed) income. See *Zero Coupon Bond*.

Default

A breach of the terms of a bond issue, eg, inability to pay interest when due.

Deferred Annuity

Annuity which does not start immediately.

Deferred Liabilities

Obligations that are repayable after more than one year. The main categories are the longer term borrowings of the company or the bonds issued by the company.

Deferred Share

A class of share where the holder is entitled to a dividend only if the ordinary shareholders have been paid a specified minimum dividend.

Defined Benefit Scheme

A pension scheme in which the rules define the benefits to be paid. Normally such schemes pay benefits based on a member's final pensionable earnings and number of years' service and are often known as final salary schemes.

Defined Contribution Scheme
A scheme where the contributions made by employer and employee are agreed and benefits are normally based on the accumulated funds and the annuity purchased with them. An alternative term is money purchase scheme.

DEL
The basic CREST transaction type for a simple (one–to–one) delivery, involving a transfer of stock, stock and cash, or cash between two CREST members.

Delivery
The satisfying of an assignment in either a put or call option by delivery of stock. Alternatively, the settlement of a futures contract during delivery month.

Deliveries by Value (DBV)
A CREST transaction, created by matching instructions, in which a package of securities up to a nominated value is transferred as overnight collateral between a borrower and lender. The transaction is for same–day settlement with collateral being returned the next morning.

Delivery by Value Return (DBR)
A set of special transactions created automatically by CREST at the settlement of a delivery by value (DBV), with a settlement date of the following day.

Delivery versus Payment (DVP)
The simultaneous and irrevocable transfer of ownership of an asset in exchange for the equivalent assured countervalue in same day funds.

Delta
The amount by which an options price will move for a given movement in the underlying asset. Also known as the hedge ratio.

Dematerialisation
Replacement of paper share certificates by electronic storage eg. CREST.

Dematerialised
The term used to describe stock which is held in electronic accounts, rather than issue paper certificates.

Department of Trade and Industry (DTI)
The Government department to which insurance companies must make regular returns under the Insurance Companies Act 1982 and the Insurance Companies (Accounts and Statements) Regulations 1983. The DTI is responsible for regulating and monitoring insurance business in the UK. These responsibilities will pass to the Financial Services Authority.

Depositary (Depository)
An organisation such as a bank or insurance company designated as an authorised person in whom property of a UK OEIC is entrusted. Broadly similar to a trustee of a unit trust.

Deposit Linking
A facility which enables a CREST member (typically a broker) to link a standard intra–CREST delivery (typically to a market maker) to particular physical transfers into the CREST system.

Deposit Protection Fund
Fund set up under the Banking Act 1975 to pay compensation in respect of deposits held by a bank which goes into liquidation.

Deposit Set
A group of documents, including transfer form and stock (ie, either certificate or certified transfer form), used for settling a sold bargain involving certificated holdings.

Depository Trust Corporation (DTC)
A depository for USA company shares.

Derivative
An instrument whose price is derived from, and dependent upon, the price of an underlying asset, encompassing options, futures or contracts for differences.

Designated Investment Exchange (DIE)
Overseas exchange recognised by the Financial Services Authority as having sufficiently similar standards (efficiency, transparency, liquidity, etc) to those of Recognised Investment Exchanges.

Designated Nominee Account
Individual beneficial owners' securities are registered in the name of the nominee company and will have a designation added. This designation identifies the beneficial owner e.g. ABC Nominees Ltd (AO1 account).

Designated Time Net Settlement (DNS)
The settlement of payment obligations at an agreed time or times on a net basis

Difference Account
Sets out details of a derivatives transaction, (difference = profit or loss).

Dilution
An increase in the number of shares issued by a company will reduce the earnings per share.

Dilution Levy
An ACD may be permitted to require payment of a dilution levy because of reduction in value of OEIC property as a result of costs incurred in dealing in investments and any spread between buying and selling prices.

Direct Offer Advertisement
An advertisement which invites investors to enter into an investment agreement, and specifies how such a response is to be made.

Direct Securities Lending
Securities lending takes place between the institution holding the securities and the borrower.

Direction
A mandatory warning issued by the SFA Investigation Department when a breach of rules has either occurred or might occur.

Directors' Model Code
The Stock Exchange Model Code for Securities transactions by directors of listed companies. This will stipulate that a company director may not deal in company shares at certain times.

Dirty Price
Price at which a bond transaction is settled, which is the clean price plus or minus an adjustment for accrued interest.

Discount
The amount by which an option or a future trades below its fair value. See *Backwardation*.

Discount Rate
The percentage rate used to calculate the present value of a future cash flow.

Discretionary Customers
Customers who entrust their funds to a firm which is then empowered to invest them without subsequent discussion with the customer. Full customer documentation is required.

Discretionary Fund Management
The investing of clients' money by a member firm on a discretionary basis, ie, customers' specific approval is not needed. Instead, customer leaves specific decisions to manager's discretion.

Discretionary Securities Lending
The custodian initiates all lending activities without referral to the beneficial owner.

Disqualification Notice
Notice issued by FSA on an individual prohibiting him from working for anyone conducting investment business.

Distributable Profits
The profits of a company available for payment to the shareholders as a dividend comprises realised profits.

Diversification
Investment technique of spreading available money over a range of investments to reduce risk.

Dividend/Distribution
A payment made to shareholders/unit holders out of the underlying companies' earnings. Dividends/distributions received in a PEP/ISA may be paid out or reinvested within the plan.

Dividend Yield
The dividend yield is the relationship between the dividend per share and the share price. The yield in general relates to a measurement of the return from an investment to its current market price, and is expressed as a percentage. The different types of yield simply use different measurements of the return.

A dividend yield is defined as:

$$\frac{\text{Dividend per share}}{\text{Current market price per share}} \times 100\%$$

For example, the dividend yield for ordinary shares for XYZ Ltd is as follows:

Dividend per share:

$$\frac{\text{Ordinary dividend}}{\text{Number of shares}}$$

$$= \frac{\$4.0m}{12m}$$

$$= \$0.33 \text{ per share}$$

The dividend yield is therefore:

$$\frac{\$0.33 \text{ (Dividend per share)}}{\$11.0 \text{ (Current market price per share)}} \times 100\%$$

$$= \underline{3.0\%}$$

DNS
See *Designated Time Net Settlement*.

DOL
See *Daily Official List*.

Domestic Bond
A bond issued in the domestic market by a domestic issuer in the domestic currency.

Double Option Agreement
An agreement between partners or shareholder directors whereby a deceased person's estate has the option to sell his share and the surviving partners have the option to buy his share. It has the same effect as a buy and sell agreement but the business assets will qualify for Inheritance Tax business property relief.

Dow Jones Average
Main share index of share prices used in the USA. Dow Jones compiles daily indices of the share prices quoted on NYSE.

Down tick
The last trade in a share is a price lower than the one before.

Drawee
The person on whom a bill of exchange is drawn.

Drawer
The person who initiates a bill of exchange, which is sent to the drawee for him to acknowledge the debt.

Drawing
A partial redemption of bonds by drawing lots.

Dread Disease
See *Critical Illness Policy*.

Drop Lock FRN
An FRN which converts into another FRN or fixed rate bond once a trigger rate has been reached.

Drop Number
A digit at the end of an identifying reference (eg, bargain reference) which signifies that the transaction is logically associated with an earlier transaction that has the same reference less the identifying digit.

Dual Currency
A bond denominated in one currency with a coupon and/or maturity value payable in another currency at a predetermined exchange rate.

Dual input transaction
CREST transactions that require input and matching of instructions by two parties. Also known as a matchable transaction.

Due Diligence
The appraisal of a business before it floats on the stock exchange, or changes ownership in a Corporate Finance deal carried out by Accountants.

Duration
Measure of the remaining life of bond adjusting for the impact of the coupon.

DVP
See *Delivery versus Payment*.

E

Early Leaver
A person who leaves a pension scheme before normal retirement without being provided with immediate retirement benefits.

Earnings
This is a company's net profit after tax, less minority interests and preference dividends. In other words it is the profit available for equity holders.

Earnings Cap
A limit to the pensionable earnings on which pension contributions attract tax relief under exempt approved schemes.

Earnings per share (EPS)
EPS shows the amount of profit earned by the company for each ordinary share. The standard definition is:

$$\frac{\text{Profit after tax and preference dividends}}{\text{Number of ordinary shares in issue}}$$

EPS is therefore the profit available to the ordinary shareholder after the deduction of all costs, taxes and preference dividends, and represents the maximum amount which could be paid out as a dividend from this year's profits.

EASDAQ
European Association of Securities Dealers Automated Quotation System. Provides a service for high potential growth European companies similar to NASDAQ in the USA.

EBS
See *Electronic Broking Service.*

ECA Regulations
The Open Ended Investment Companies (Investment Companies with Variable Capital) Regulations, 1996. They are known as ECA Regulations because they were enacted under the European Communities Act 1972.

ECHO
The Exchange Clearing House: a multi–lateral foreign exchange netting system.

ECSDA
European Central Securities Depository Association, of which CREST is the UK member.

ECU
European Unit of Account. A so–called 'basket currency' made up of the EU currencies. The forerunner of the euro used by the European Commission for accounting purposes and also for financial transactions such as bond issues and loans.

Economic & Monetary Union (EMU)
The system that links together the economies and currencies of the participating Euro countries. In January 1999, exchange rates were linked, the Euro became a currency in its own right and the European Central Bank became responsible for centralised monetary policy.

EDSP
Exchange Delivery Settlement Price is the exchange designated settlement price for delivery (or cash settlement) of the underlying instrument.

Efficient Portfolio
A portfolio which achieves a given return at the lowest risk or which achieves the highest return for a given level of risk.

EGM
Extraordinary General Meeting of a company's shareholders.

Electronic Broking Service (EBS)
An automated broking system for dealing in currency. EBS was formed in 1993.

Electronic Order Book
The electronic order matching system used as the system for dealing in the shares which comprise the FT–SE 100 index.

Eligible Bill
A bill of exchange which the Bank of England will take as security when acting as 'lender of last resort' to the banking system.

Eligible Market
A securities market in which a unit trust can invest. Either a market within the EU on which transferable securities are traded or any other

market agreed between the unit trust manager and the trustee because it meets certain criteria, e.g. adequate liquidity.

Emerging Markets
A term which refers to newer securities markets. Generally these may be relatively illiquid, under–regulated, with poor settlement systems etc. but have attracted high levels of cross–border investment because of their perceived long–term attractions.

Emerging Markets Clearing Corporation
A clearing house for emerging markets securities used by market dealers and brokers.

Emerging Markets Traders Association
An association of investment banks involved in emerging markets trading activities.

EMU
See *Economic & Monetary Union*.

Endowment
A life policy which pays out on maturity or earlier in the case of death.

Endowment Mortgage
Form of mortgage where the lender is only paid the interest on the loan and a separate endowment policy is taken out to provide sufficient funds to repay the loan on maturity.

Endowment Policy
Form of saving linked in with life assurance. Must be held for at least 10 years to get full benefit.

Enforcement Inspectors
SFA employees working within the Monitoring Department. Powers include entering any member firm's office without notice, interviewing any member of staff, and copying any document or computer record.

Enfranchisement
A corporate action in which a company extends voting rights to a non-voting or restricted voting class of shares.

Enhanced Scrip Dividend
To enable a company to save tax, it may offer its shareholders shares instead of a cash dividend but in the form of an Enhanced Scrip which is a scrip dividend option with a guaranteed cash sale option where the sale proceeds exceed the cash dividend and the related tax credit.

Enterprise Investment Scheme (EIS)
Replaced the BES for new shares issued after 31 December 1993 in qualifying companies. Investors can claim income tax relief at 20% on qualifying investments up to £100,000 in any tax year, and also claim 'roll-over' relief for capital gains, giving a maximum effective relief of 60%.

Entitlement
See *Open Offer*.

Equalisation
A refund of a small part of the initial investment in a unit trust which investors receive with their first income distribution. Paid on 'Group 2' units.

Equity Shares
Shares in a company that are entitled to the balance of profits and assets after all prior charges.

Equity/Stock Options
These are contracts based on individual equities or shares. On exercise of the option the specified amount of shares is exchanged between the buyer and the seller through the clearing organisation. See *Traded Options*.

Equity Index Swap
An obligation between two parties to exchange cash flows based on the percentage change in one or more stock indices, for a specific period with previously agreed reset dates. The swap is cash settled and based on notional principal amounts. One side of an equity swap can involve a LIBOR reference rate.

Equity repo
A transaction in which two parties agree that one will sell equity securities to the other and (at the same time and as part of the same transaction) commit to repurchase equivalent securities on a specified future date, or at call, at a specified price.

ERISA Funds
US domestic funds permitted under the Employee Retirement Income Security Act 1974 to diversify into non–US securities.

ERM
See *Exchange Rate Mechanism*.

ERNIE (Electronic Random Number Indicator Equipment)
Colloquial name for the computer which selects the winners of premium bonds prizes.

ESCB
European System of Central Banks.

Escrow Account
An account controlled by a third party into which a buyer places funds or other assets (eg shares) to meet a commitment, pending specified actions by the seller. In CREST, when a corporate action involves acceptance of an offer, the affected dematerialised stock is transferred by the accepting holder into a special escrow account within the Receiving Agent's membership. The stock remains in the name of the holder, but is under the control of the receiving (escrow) agent. An escrow account can also be used to place stock under the control of a bank, to give effect to an equitable mortgage.

ESO
European Settlements Office. Now defunct, this unit was run by the Bank of England to hold ECU denominated instruments, which are now held in CMO, Euroclear or Cedel.

ESOS
Executive share option schemes.

ETD
This is the common term used to describe Exchange-Traded Derivatives which are standardised products. It differentiates products which are listed on an exchange as opposed to those offered Over-The-Counter (OTC).

EURIBOR
A rate used for Euro interest rate fixings based upon dealings in the markets of Euro zone.

Euro
The name of the new European currency to be used in the countries within the Economic and Monetary Union. The countries which joined on 1st January 1999 were: Austria, Belgium, Finland, France, Germany, Ireland, Italy, Luxembourg, Netherlands, Portugal and Spain.

EURO LIBOR
A rate used for Euro interest rate fixings based upon dealings in the London market.

Eurobond
A negotiable debt security issued outside the country of its currency and intended for international distribution.

Euroclear
Founded in 1968 Euroclear provides clearing, settlement and custody for a wide range of internationally traded eurobonds, domestic bonds and equities. Euroclear is one of two International Central Securities Depositories; the other being Cedel.

Eurocommercial Paper
Commercial paper denominated in a currency other than that of the country in which the issuer is based.

Eurocurrency
A currency held on deposit in a country other than its country of origin.

Eurodollar
A US–denominated deposit located in a bank outside the United States.

Euromarket
An international market with no central location where organisations invest in international securities such as eurobonds, international/foreign bonds, warrants, convertibles, etc. The unofficial headquarters is generally recognised to be London.

European Council
Made up of EU heads of State plus the President of the European Commission.

European Depositary Receipts
Used to deal in UK, US and Japanese stocks, traded in bearer form on European markets.

European Monetary System (EMS)
Agreement between most members of the common market on how to organise their currencies. Superseded by Economic and Monetary Union.

European Style Option
An option that can only be exercised on the expiry date in contrast with an American Style Option.

Ex
Indication that the seller retains the right to any benefits and entitlements; consequently the buyer does not receives them. See *Cum*.

Ex–Date
The date specified by the local stock exchange used to determine whether the buyer or seller of the security is entitled to the benefit. The seller of a security during the ex period will normally be entitled to the benefit.

Ex–Dividend or Ex–Distribution (XD)
This means that the seller of a security is entitled to the next distribution and the buyer is not.

Ex–Dividend or Ex–Distribution Price
A price which entitles a seller of units to the next income payment. A fund with an ex–dividend price is denoted in the financial press by xd. Where xd is not quoted on the contract note it is assumed it is cum–div and the buyer will receive the distribution. (Such notation will not appear on accumulation unit contracts.)

Ex–Dividend/Distribution – Purchase/Sale
Shares/units purchased will not be entitled to the next dividend. Shares/units sold will be entitled to the next dividend.

Ex–Period
During a benefit distribution, the period between the ex date and payment date during which the seller will normally be entitled to the benefit, unless specifically agreed otherwise in the terms of the trade.

Ex–Rights Price
Share price after a rights issue. Shares sold without the entitlement to the rights.

Ex–Scrip Price
Share price after a scrip issue.

Exchange
A market place where any form of trading takes place.

Exchange Delivery Settlement Price (EDSP)
The price determined by the exchange for physical delivery of the underlying instrument or cash settlement.

Exchange Price Feeds
The link from exchanges to information providers which gives information on dealings.

Exchange Rate
The rate at which one currency trades against another.

Exchange Rate Mechanism (ERM)
A system of adjustable exchange rates used by certain European countries whereby currencies operated within defined exchange rate bands. Superseded by Economic and Monetary Union.

Exchange–Owned Clearing Organisation
Exchange– (or member–) owned clearing organisations are structured so that the clearing members guarantee each other. A members' default fund and additional funding like insurance provide mutual cover, with no independent guarantee.

Execute and eliminate order
Type of order input into SETS. The amount that can be matched immediately against displayed orders is completed, with the remainder being rejected.

Execution
The action of trading in the markets.

Execution and Clearing Agreement
An agreement signed between the buyer/seller and the clearing broker. This agreement sets out the terms by which the clearing broker will conduct business with the buyer/seller.

Execution Only
Instructions to buy or sell, given directly by the investor to the broker, without receiving any advice.

Execution Only or Give–Up Agreement
Tri–partite agreements which are signed by the executing broker, the clearing broker and the client. This agreement sets out the terms by which the clearing broker will accept business on behalf of the client.

Execution–Only Customers
Customers who do not want the firm's advice but wish to be able to execute transactions by instructing the firm.

Executive Pension Plan (EPP)
An individual money purchase arrangement, normally for senior executives and directors. EPPs are usually provided by insurance companies.

Exempt Approved Scheme
An Inland Revenue approved scheme (not a personal pension) which provides the tax relief set out in Taxes Act 1988.

Exempt Trusts/Funds
Unit trusts and investment funds only open for investments from Charities and Pension Funds. These tax–exempt bodies are not liable to either UK income or Capital Gains Tax (CGT).

Exercise
Procedure whereby the owner of an option takes up his rights.

Exercise an option
Take up the right to buy or sell the stock which is the subject of the option.

Exercise Price
The fixed price, per share or unit, at which an option conveys the right to call (purchase) or put (sell) the underlying shares or units.

Exit Charges
With effect from 1st November 1994, under revised FSA regulations, unit trust managers have been given the option to levy a charge on redemption of units in place of, or in combination with, their initial charge. This new charge is referred to as an exit charge. Because it is levied on the bid value and initial charges on creation value, a 4.762% exit charge equates to a 5% initial charge.

Expert Customer
A client who is considered experienced enough to be treated as a Non-private Customer.

Expiry Date
The last date on which option holders can exercise their right. After this date an option is deemed to lapse or be abandoned.

Extraordinary General Meeting (EGM)
A meeting of shareholders which is held by a company on an ad hoc basis for a particular purpose. A period of notice (usually 14 or 21 days) must be given.

F

Face Value
See *Nominal*.

Factfind
The questionnaire created by most financial advisers and sellers of insurance products or packaged products to find out the details about a prospective client. Information from it provides the basis for structuring suitable advice.

Factoring
A process whereby one company takes over the responsibility of debt collection from another.

Fair Value
A mathematically calculated value for an option or future that accommodates a trader's parameters for interest rates, dividends etc. Different tax regimes or interest rate environments may give rise to different fair values for different investors in the same instrument.

False Market
See *Misleading Statement*.

Feeder Fund
A relevant pension scheme dedicated to a single regulated collective investment scheme or to a single eligible investment trust.

Foreign Income Dividends (FID)
Income paid from overseas earnings on which tax is treated as paid but on which there is no tax credit, therefore no tax may be reclaimed.

Fill or Kill order
Type of order input into SETS or the options market. It is either completed in full against displayed orders or rejected in full.

Final Dividend
The dividend paid by a company as the final payment for a particular financial year.

Final Remuneration
The maximum earnings that can be used for the purpose of calculating maximum approvable pension benefits. It may include the value of benefits–in–kind as well as salary.

Final Salary Scheme
Pension scheme where the benefit is based on the member's pensionable earnings for a period ending at or before normal retirement date or leaving service.

Financial Futures/Options Contracts
Financial futures is a term used to describe futures contracts based on financial instruments like currencies, debt instruments and financial indices. An agreement to buy or sell a fixed quantity of a specified interest rate or currency product for delivery at a fixed date in the future at a fixed price.

Financial Instruments
See *Instrument*.

Financial Services Act 1986 (FSA 86 or FSA 1986)
This act currently provides the framework for regulation of the financial services industry in the UK and a regime for the protection of investors. It is expected to be superseded by the Financial Services and Markets Act.

Financial Services Authority (FSA)
The agency designated by the DTI to regulate investment business as required by FSA 1986. It is the main regulator of the financial sector and was formerly called the Securities and Investments Board (SIB).

Financial Services Authority Core Rules
Forty rules that set out the essential requirements for investor protection and acceptable market behaviour.

Financial Services Authority Principles
Ten statements applying directly to the conduct of investment business and forming the basis of the standards that are expected from all authorised persons.

First Notice Day
The first day that the holders of short positions can give notification to the exchange/clearing house that they wish to effect delivery.

Fiscal Year
The relevant period for assessing total income and capital gains for liability to tax. Runs from 6 April in one year to 5 April in the following year.

Fit and Proper
Under FSA 86 everyone conducting investment business must be a 'fit and proper person'. The Act does not define the term, a function which is left to the regulators such as FSA or SROs.

Fixed Assets
The assets of a company acquired for long–term use within the company, for example, buildings, plant and equipment.

Fixed Exchange Rate
System whereby the rate of a country's currency is established at a particular level in relation to other currencies and is not allowed to move from that level.

Fixed Interest Securities
Also known as bonds. Securities which carry rights to a fixed rate of interest and eventual repayment of the capital sum.

Fixed Rate Borrowing
A fixed rate borrowing establishing the interest rate that will be paid throughout the life of the loan.

Fixing
The calculation of the coupon rate for a FRN covering the next coupon payment period.

Flat Position
In the options and futures markets, a position which has been fully closed out and no liability to make or take delivery exists.

Flat Yield
Also known as income yield. Income return on owning a bond. Calculated by dividing the coupon by the market price and multiplying by 100.

Flex Options
Newly introduced contracts which are a cross between OTCs and exchange traded products. The advantage of flex options is that participants can choose various parts of the contract specification such as the expiry date and exercise price.

Floating Exchange Rate
System whereby the rate of a country's currency against others is determined by market forces without any intervention from the Government.

Floating Rate Note (FRN)
Eurobonds with a rate of interest that varies from coupon period to coupon period. The rate is usually established as a margin over LIBOR.

Floor
An option which fixes the minimum interest rate receivable on a deposit/loan for a series of interest payments.

Floor Brokerage
The process of delegating the execution to another counterparty.

Flotation
The process of bringing a company's shares to the market for the first time.

Foreign Bond
Like a eurobond, it is a debt security issued by non–resident borrowers but is underwritten by a syndicate of banks composed primarily of institutions from one country. It is denominated in that country's currency and sold principally in that country.

Foreign Exchange (Forex)
A term commonly used to encompass the buying and selling of foreign currencies. 'Forex' is used as an abbreviation for foreign exchange.

Forward Contract
A contract between two counterparties where one person agrees to buy from the other person, who agrees to sell, a certain amount of a financial instrument or a commodity at a stated price but for delivery at an agreed future date.

Forward Forward
An agreement at a future date, to purchase an instrument which will mature at a period some time in the future.

Forward Market
Dealings that are made for delivery and settlement on a date other than the spot.

Forward Points
The interest rate differential between two currencies. Quoted as forward foreign exchange points or pips, and added to or taken from the spot exchange rate.

Forward Pricing
System for pricing units in a unit trust, where buyers and sellers trade on the basis of prices to be set at the next price fixing for units, ie. after an instruction from an investor has been received. cf Historic Pricing.

Forward Rate
The rate at which a foreign exchange contract is struck today for settlement at a specified future date. A compilation of the spot exchange rate plus or minus the forward points.

Forward Rate Agreement (FRA)
An agreement between two parties where the fixing of the interest rate payable or receivable at a future date on a given notional amount is set today.

Forwards
These are very similar to futures contracts but they are not normally traded on an exchange. They are not marked to market daily but settled only on the delivery date.

Franked Income
Dividends from UK companies are paid after the company has paid corporation tax. This income is referred to as 'franked'.

Free Asset Ratio
The surplus assets of a life assurance company over its liabilities in relation to its total assets. The FAR shows the company's capacity for future growth and to make future bonus payments to with–profits policyholders.

Free Money
Money held on behalf of a client under IMRO and PIA rules for safe keeping. It must be kept separate from the firm's own money and the client is usually entitled to interest on it.

Free of Payment
The movement of assets for which there is no associated (cash) countervalue. The movement of assets which is not dependent on the simultaneous payment of the cash countervalue.

Free Of Tax To Residents Abroad (FOTRA)
Gilts where the interest is paid gross to non–UK residents who will not be liable to any tax on it.

Free Standing AVC (FSAVC)
An AVC arrangement which is not directly linked to the employer's main scheme. See *AVCs*.

Friendly Societies
Organisations that are set up for the mutual benefit of their members and are non–profit making. Although the term covers building societies, co–operatives and trade unions, some friendly societies are focussed on retail financial services and offer 10 year endowment policies. There are tax benefits to the policies but only modest sums can be invested.

Friendly Society Exempt Policy
A savings policy where the fund is free of UK tax on investment income and capital gains.

FRN
See *Floating Rate Note*.

Front Office
The term used for the Trading or Dealing room.

FSA
See *Financial Services Authority*.

FSA 86 or FSA 1986
See *Financial Services Act 1986*.

FT–SE All Share Index
The Financial Times Actuaries measure of the leading 850 companies listed on the UK Stock Market.

FT–SE 100 Index
Weighted arithmetic index of the prices of the UK's leading 100 shares. It is a real time index calculated by The London Stock Exchange.

FT–SE Mid 250 Index
Index of the prices of the 250 shares below the top 100. Calculated in the same way as the FT–SE 100.

Full Arbitration Service
Provided by SFA for claims above £50,000. Involves both written and oral evidence. The arbitrator's decision is binding.

Fully Paid Shares
Shares on which no further 'call' is due. Once a call has been paid to the company for new shares offered to existing shareholders, they can be traded in the form of allotment letters until definitive certificates become available. Dealing is on a cash settlement basis. See *Record Date, Allotment Letter*.

Full Replication
A method of running an index–tracking fund in which all the shares comprising an index are held in their respective market weightings.

Fund Manager
An organisation that invests money on behalf of someone else.

Fund of Funds
Authorised unit trust which invests in the units of other unit trusts.

Fundamental analysis
Detailed analysis of a company and the industry in which it operates to identify whether the shares are over – or undervalued.

Funded Debt
Short–term debt converted into long–term debt.

Funded Pension Scheme
A pension fund set up by a company to provide pensions for employees who have retired. The company, and possibly the employee, pay contributions to be invested in the fund during the employee's working life.

Fungible
Able to be co–mingled, identical securities in a bookkeeping system in which no specific securities are assigned by serial number to any one holder's account. See *Non–Fungible*.

Fungible Bonds
An interchangeable pool of securities of the same security code from which deliveries are made without reference to any particular identifiable certificate. See *Non–Fungible*.

Future
A futures contract is a legally binding arrangement by which one party commits to buying a standard quantity and quality of an asset from another party on a specified date in the future, but at a price agreed today. The counterparty is obliged to sell the asset at the agreed price and agreed date. Because the price is agreed at the outset the seller (buyer) is protected from a fall (rise) in the price of the underlying in the intervening time period.

Futures and Options Fund
A unit trust scheme dedicated to approved and other derivatives (where most or all the transactions are fully covered by cash, securities or other derivatives), whether with or without transferable securities.

Future Value
The equivalent value in the future of having a set sum of money or stream of cash flows.

G

G30 (Group Of Thirty)
A private sector group concerned with the workings of the international financial system.

G30 Recommendations
Nine recommendations made in 1989 by the G30 to improve the Clearing and Settlement Systems in the world's securities markets and thus reduce risk and increase efficiency.

Geared Futures and Options Fund (GFOF)
A unit trust dedicated to approved and other derivatives where most or all of the extent of investment is limited by the amount of property available to be put up as initial outlay, whether with or without transferable securities.

Gearing

The proportion of the assets that have been funded from borrowing and the proportion funded by the shareholders. A common measurement is the debt/equity ratio defined as:

$$\frac{\text{Profit}}{\text{Shareholders' Funds}} \times 100\%$$

The US expression for Gearing is Leverage.

GDP

See *Gross Domestic Product*.

General Principles

10 fundamental principles written by FSA to apply to all investment businesses.

Gilt Edged Market Makers (GEMMs)

A firm that is a market maker in gilts and is not permitted to do much else. Also known as a primary dealer.

Gilts

Abbreviated name for gilt edged securities which are UK government issued fixed interest securities or index–linked securities.

Give Up

The process of giving a trade to a third party who will undertake the clearing and settlement of the trade.

Global Bond

Bonds distributed in both the Euromarkets and in one or more domestic markets.

Global Clearing
The channelling of the settlement of all futures and options trades through a single counterparty or through a number of counterparties geographically located.

Global Custodian
A global custodian provides clients with multi–currency custody, settlement and reporting services which extend beyond the global custodian's and client's base region and currency; and encompasses all classes of financial instruments.

GLOBEX
The overnight trading system operated by Reuters and the Chicago Mercantile Exchange (CME), which was developed in 1992.

GMP
See *Guaranteed Minimum Pension*.

Good for The Day (GTD)
A limit order which expires at the end of the day if it has not been executed.

Good Till Cancelled (GTC)
A limit order which stays effective until either it executes or is deleted by the broker which placed it.

Government Bonds
Bonds issued by a government to finance its borrowing requirements.

Grey Market
Forward trading in new issues between market participants during the period from the announcement of a new issue to the closing date. Trades are dealt on a 'when issued' basis to cover the possibility that the issue might be withdrawn.

Gross
1. Before tax has been paid.
2. A position which is held with both the bought and sold trades kept open.

Gross Domestic Product (GDP)
Measure of a country's output which calculates the value of goods produced within that country.

Gross Income Yield
The income return on an investment before tax has been deducted.

Gross National Product (GNP)
Measure of a country's output comprising GDP as adjusted for net inflows or outflows of income with other countries.

Gross Redemption Yield (GRY)
The Gross Redemption Yield (or Yield to Maturity) of a bond is the return a bond earns on the price at which it was purchased if held to maturity. The calculation takes into account any capital gain or loss over the full period and assumes that all interest payments are reinvested at the yield to maturity. (In the case of index linked bonds, the redemption price and future interest payments are not known so certain standard assumptions are made regarding future inflation rates)..

Group
Where one company controls one or more other companies, they are collectively a group.

Group Personal Pension (GPP)
An arrangement made for the employees of a particular employer to participate in a personal pension scheme on a grouped basis. GPPs are not separate schemes, merely collecting arrangements.

Growth Stock
Shares in a company with a low dividend yield and high investor expectations of future growth.

Guaranteed Annuity
Annuity which is guaranteed to make payments for a minimum period even if the annuitant dies during that period. Payments continue after that period if the annuitant is still alive.

Guaranteed Income/Growth Bond
Normally single premium life assurance policies that provide a guaranteed fixed level of income or growth over a pre-determined period.

Guaranteed Minimum Pension (GMP)
The minimum pension which an occupational pension scheme has to provide as one of the conditions for contracting out of SERPS, unless it is contracted out through providing protected rights. For employees leaving service within two years of joining, their employer's scheme can pay a contributions equivalent premium to the State scheme to buy them back into SERPS. Employees with over two years service in the scheme have to be granted a preserved pension revalued in line with the National Average Price Index.

GUI
Graphical User Interface. The term GUI is used to refer to the Windows™ based system supplied by CRESTCo which allows interactive connection to CREST or CGO via one of the approved networks.

H

Hang Seng Index
Index of the Hong Kong Stock Exchange.

Hard Commodities
Commodities such as tin or zinc. Futures on them are generally traded on the London Metal Exchange.

Hard Currency
A currency whose exchange rate seems to be rising against other currencies. See *Soft Currency*.

Headroom
The credit that is available to a member during the CREST processing day, based on the difference between the member's credit limit (ie, cap) and its net payment obligation. Headroom (and the cap) is dynamic, varying throughout the day as the result of transactions settling.

Hedge Ratio
See *Delta*.

Hedging
Use of investments to protect or minimise a potential loss to an existing position or known commitment.

Historic Pricing
System for pricing units where buyers and sellers trade on the basis of prices set at the last price fix before their dealing instruction was received. cf Forward Pricing. Contrast with forward pricing.

Historic Volatility
The standard deviation of the change in the price of the underlying over a designated time period.

Holder (Options)
The beneficial or legal owner of an asset. Buyer of an option. See *Writer*.

Holding Company
A company which owns more than 50% of the shares of another company is its holding company.

Home State regulation
Under the Investment Services Directive (ISD), an investment business is authorised in the place of its head office and registered office. This home state authorisation entitles it to conduct business in any member state of the European Union.

Host State
Under the ISD any member of the European Union where an investment business established in any other EU state is now conducting business.

Host State regulation
Any European investment business operating outside its home basis is regulated by its host for its Conduct of Business.

Hybrid Security
A security that has the characteristics of both debt and equity.

I

ICAEW
Institute of Chartered Accountants in England and Wales. The RPB responsible for chartered accountants.

ICSA
Institute of Chartered Secretaries and Administrators, the professional body of company secretaries and registrars.

Identification Rules
Rules which determine which shares are deemed to be sold for Capital Gains Tax purposes, when only part of a holding is being sold.

IFA
See *Independent Financial Adviser.*

Immobilised Securities
Securities which are stored collectively in a vault in order to eliminate physical movement of securities or documents of title when transfer of ownership takes place. All movements of immobilised securities subsequently occur by book entry transfer.

Implied Volatility
The level of volatility that the current market price of a derivative is implying.

IMRO
See *Investment Management Regulatory Organisation*.

In–The–Money Warrant
A warrant with intrinsic value.

Inc.
A US corporation.

Income
Dividends or distributions received from an investment.

Income Allocation Date
Date by which income attributable to units in authorised trusts must have been computed and dispatched to unit holders.

Income Bonds (National Savings)
National Savings product which pays regular income.

Income Share
Income shareholders in an investment trust company have the right to all the income received from the underlying portfolio and distributed as dividends and a fixed repayment of capital when the company is wound up.

Income Statement
See *Profit and Loss Account*.

Income Stock
Shares which yield above average income. Normally the basis for income unit trusts. Also known as blue chip stock.

Income Tax
The tax that is charged on all income as defined by tax laws. Includes dividends, interest, rental income, pension receipts and retirement annuities receipts.

Income Units
Investors holding such units are entitled to receive regular income payments. The payments are usually made twice a year, but can be quarterly or monthly. See *Income Allocation Dates*.

Income Yield
See *Flat Yield*.

Indemnity Guarantee Policy
Insurance taken out by mortgage providers to cover loans which represent a high percentage of the purchase price of a property.

Independence Policy
SFA practice which ensures customers' interests are put first if a conflict of interest should arise.

Independent Clearing Organisation
The independent organisation is quite separate from the actual members of the exchange and will guarantee, to each member, the performance of the contracts by having them registered in the organisation's name.

Independent Financial Adviser (IFA)
Adviser not employed by a single firm who can select from all companies' products ie. pensions, unit trusts etc when providing 'best advice' to their client.

Index
A figure calculated from the share prices of a specific number of shares on a Stock Exchange.

Index Arbitrage
The purchase or sale of a basket of different shares and the simultaneous sale or purchase of an index derivative based on the shares in the basket.

Index Fund
Also known as a tracker fund and is a type of unit trust which invests in the component parts of a particular index. Charges tend to be relatively low.

Index-Linked Bonds
Bonds which have their coupon and principal index linked, usually to the Retail Price Index. The return on the bond will therefore rise in line with inflation.

Index-Linked Gilts
Gilt edged securities where both the annual interest and the capital at redemption are revalued in line with the Retail Prices Index.

Indirect Customer
These are clients who carry on business with an SFA firm through an intermediary or agent. Where an agent identifies their client, this obliges the member firm to treat the client as its indirect customer and apply the SFA customer rules to the client instead of the agent.

Individual Savings Account (ISA)
Introduced in April 1999 and have taken the place of Personal Equity Plans (PEPs) and TESSAs. An ISA is a scheme of investment with no tax liability on income or capital gains tax arising from assets held within the scheme. It is not an investment in itself, but a wrapper put around one or more investments, and may comprise of components which fluctuate in value eg. stocks and shares.

Industrial Assurance
A class of business where the premiums are physically collected in cash from the policyholder by an agent of the life office.

Inflation
A persistent rise in prices in an economy.

Inflation Risk
The risk that the real value of an investment and its income falls because of inflation.

Inheritance Tax (IHT)
The tax that is levied on a person's estate after their death.

Initial Charge
The initial charge on a unit trust is made when the units are sold to the investor. The charge is a percentage of the bid price, and covers the manager's start–up costs including commissions.

Initial Margin
Collateral deposited when opening a position (eg writing an option or trading a future).

Initial Public Offering (IPO)
The primary market of the stock market. See *Primary Market*.

Initial Offer Price
The price at which units are available to the public in a new trust for a limited period which may not exceed 21 days.

Initial Yield
An estimated figure which indicates how much income a new unit trust buyer might expect to receive in the first year of his investment. This is not the only basis of preparing an estimate. Estimated gross yield is calculated before allowing for tax credit amounts.

'In specie' Dealings
An ACD can arrange for the issue of shares in return for certain investments, and this, for example, would be a method of converting an investment trust into an OEIC. Similarly, the ACD can agree with a shareholder for shares to be redeemed by way of a transfer of a suitable proportion of the OEIC's portfolio of equal value.

Insider Dealing (Criminal Justice Act 1993)
A crime committed when an individual in possession of unpublished price sensitive information and knowingly connected with a company attempts to deal in its shares; or when the information is communicated to a third party in the expectation that it will be acted upon.

Institutional Investor
An organisation whose primary purpose is to invest its own assets or those managed on behalf of others. Includes pension funds, investment companies, insurance companies and banks.

Instrument
Used to describe a form of financing mechanism such as bonds, bills of exchange etc. The term is normally used to describe the actual document.

Instrument of Incorporation
Legal document which sets out the constitution of and internal regulations of an OEIC. Broadly similar to a Companies Act company's memorandum and articles of association.

Intramarket Spread
Two futures over the same underlying with different maturity dates are traded – one is bought and the other is sold.

Insurable Interest
A legally recognised interest enabling a person to insure another. The insured must stand to be financially worse off on the death of the life assured to an extent capable of valuation and as a result of a legally recognised relationship.

Intended Settlement Date (ISD)
The date on which a transaction will settle, if the associated stock and/or cash is available. Abbreviated as ISD.

Interbank Market
A market in which banks deal between themselves (see LIBOR).

Interbank Rate
Interest rates at which banks will take and place cash deposits with each other. Other forms of borrowing might be based on these interbank rates. See *LIBOR, LIBID, EUROIBOR.*

Interest
Payment made for the use of money over time.

Interest In Possession
Broadly, the legal right to income from, or enjoyment of trust property.

Interest Payment
A benefit distribution in which a cash payment is made to holders of certain types of stock issued by the company. The rate of interest and the interval for payment are determined within the original terms of issue of the stock. The company's agent pays the interest on the dates specified by these terms.

Interest Rate Futures
Based on a debt instrument such as a Government Bond or a Treasury Bill as the underlying product and require the delivery of a bond or bill to fulfil the contract.

Interest Rate Risk
The risk that the value of a fixed interest security will fall with a rise in interest rates. It is also the risk that the income from a variable interest investment will fall with a fall in interest rates.

Interest Rate Parity
Formula, based on the interest rate differential between two currencies, which calculates the theoretical forward exchange rate.

Interest Rate Swap (IRS)
An agreement to exchange interest related payments in the same currency from fixed rate into floating rate (or vice versa) or from one type of floating rate to another.

Interest Yield
See *Flat Yield*.

Interim Accounting Period
One or more periods ending on dates prior to the end of the fund's annual accounting period in respect of which interim distributions of income are paid.

Interim Bonus
The bonus rate applying to claims that arise before the next official declaration date.

Interim Dividend
A dividend paid by a company during the course of its financial year. See *Final Dividend*.

Intermediaries Offer
A system for primary issues on the London Stock Exchange. Stock is made available to brokers who can take it on behalf of clients.

Intermediary
Financial adviser/solicitor, etc.

International Bank for Reconstruction and Development (IBRD)
An international organisation established at Bretton Woods, to control the financial requirements for the re-building of war-torn Europe. Its function has evolved into financing the development of LDCs. Now known as the World Bank.

International Central Securities Depository (ICSD)
A CSD established to provide settlements and custody services for domestic (CSD) and foreign securities. The two ICSDs are Cedel and Euroclear.

International Equity
An equity of a company based outside the UK but traded internationally.

International Monetary Fund
An organisation set up by Bretton Woods to oversee the fixed exchange rate regime (now defunct) and to provide borrowing facilities to allow corrective action to be taken to alleviate exchange rate pressure in deficit countries.

International Organisation for Standardisation (ISO)
A worldwide federation of national standards bodies mandated to develop and promulgate standards for communications, including various numbering systems associated with international commerce. See *British Standards Institution*.

International Petroleum Exchange (IPE)
Market place for trading energy product derivatives.

International Primary Markets Association (IPMA)
A professional association which oversees the market practices and procedures for the primary or new issue eurobond markets.

International Securities Identification Number (ISIN)
A coding system developed by ISO with the purpose of creating one unique number on a global basis for identifying securities.

International Securities Markets Association (ISMA)
Founded in 1969 as the Association of International Bond Dealers, ISMA is both a Designated Investment Exchange (under FSA) and an International Securities Self Regulatory Organisation (under FSA 1986). ISMA supervises the activities of over 900 members in 30 countries.

International Securities Services Association (ISSA)
An organisation consisting of international banks, ISSA was set-up in 1979 to promote progress in worldwide securities administration. (Formerly known until May 1996 as the International Society of Securities Administrators.)

International Swaps and Dealers Association (ISDA)
The trade body for derivatives dealers.

Intervention
The process whereby the Bank of England acts to influence the exchange rate for sterling by buying it to support its value or selling to weaken it.

Intervention Order
Notice from an SRO to one of its members where immediate action is required to prevent serious damage being done.

Intestate
Deceased person not having made a will.

In-The-Money
Any option with intrinsic value. For a call the strike price will be below the current market price (of the underlying stock) and for a put the strike will be above the current market price.

Intra-Day Exposure
See *Daylight Exposure*

Intra-Day Margin
An extra margin call which the clearing organisation can call during the day when there is a very large movement up or down in the price of the contract.

Intrinsic Value
The amount an option would be worth if it expired immediately. This will come to either the positive difference between the strike and the underlying price, or zero.

Investigation
Carried out by the SFA Investigations Department when a member firm is suspected of misconduct by the Monitoring Department.

Investment Advertisement
Announcement inviting persons to enter into an investment agreement.

Investment Bank
A bank specialising in capital market dealing, origination and distribution and in corporate finance activities

Investment Business
Dealing, advising or managing investments. Those doing so need to be authorised.

Investment Management Regulatory Organisation (IMRO)
Investment Management Regulatory Organisation Limited is the self regulatory organisation which regulates the activities of fund managers, unit trust groups, occupational pension funds, merchant banks, clearing banks and venture capitalists.

Investment Ombudsman
Part of the regulatory complaints procedure. The ombudsman deals with complaints against members of IMRO, which the member has been unable to resolve. These may include claims of negligence and breach of contract.

Investment Services Directive (ISD)
European Union Directive implemented in the UK in January 1996, the objective of which is to harmonise standards of regulation and therefore allow firms established in any EU member state to conduct investment business in any other EU state.

Investment Specific Risk
The risks associated with a particular investment. Diversification is used to reduce it. This risk is separate from market risk.

Investment Trust (Company)
Quoted companies which invest in the shares of other companies. They are close-ended so their market value can be less (at a discount) than net asset value. They can also be more (at a premium) than net asset value.

Investments
General meaning is any products in which money is spent with the aim of receiving more money back at a later date. FSA 1986 defines it more specifically and only those activities so defined are regulated by the Act.

Investment Protection Committee (IPC)
Divisions of the ABI and NAPF set up to monitor their positions as shareholders.

Investors Compensation Scheme
Scheme run by FSA to compensate private customers in the event of the default of the authorised investment business through whom they invested. Only applies in respect of FSA 1986 regulated products and firms.

Investors Protection Scheme
Fund set up under the Building Societies Act 1986 to pay compensation in respect of deposits held at a building society that goes into liquidation.

Invoice Amount
The amount calculated under the formula specified by the exchange which will be paid in settlement of the delivery of the underlying asset.

Irish Stock Exchange
A Recognised Investment Exchange (RIE), providing a market place for Irish registered securities.

Irredeemable Stock
A fixed interest stock (eg, gilts) which shows no date at which the government have to redeem it.

Irrevocable Payment
A payment instruction that cannot be cancelled by the sender.

ISA
See *Individual Savings Account*.

ISD
See *Intended Settlement Date*. Also abbv. for Investment Services Directive.

ISIN
See *International Securities Identification Number (ISIN)*.

ISITC
Industry Standardisation for Institutional Trade Communications group. Set up to standardise communication between Fund Managers and their Custodians.

ISO
See *International Organisation for Standardisation (ISO)*.

Issue Price
The price at which a new issue is fixed.

Issuer
An entity (Sovereign, country, supranational, banking or corporate) that raises cash through issuing negotiable securities.

Issuing
The process an institution will go though for the issuance of debt paper.

J

Japan Securities Depository Centre (JASDEC)
A central depository for Japanese shares, similar to the US DTC.

JGB
Japanese government bond.

Joint Life Policy
Life policies jointly effected by two life assureds, usually husband and wife.

Junk Bond
High–risk bonds which have a poor credit rating with a relatively high risk of default. Coupon rates are therefore higher than would be expected for creditworthy borrowers.

K

Kassenverein
Depository banks for securities within the German clearing system.

Key Features Document
A document drawn up for all potential investors containing essential information about an OEIC to enable them to determine whether they should invest and what their rights are.

Key Person Insurance
Insurance of a person who is vital to the continued profitability of a business.

Know Your Customer
The duty to ascertain sufficient information about a customer to enable suitable advice to be given.

L

Lapsed Rights
In a rights issue, rights for which call payments have not been made by acceptance date.

Last Notice Day
The final day that notification of delivery will be possible. On most exchanges all outstanding short futures contracts are automatically delivered to open long positions.

Last Trading Day
Often the day preceding last notice day which is the final opportunity for holders of long positions to trade out of their positions and avoid ultimate delivery.

Launch
The announcement that a new bond is to be issued.

LCH
The London Clearing House, which acts as central counterparty to all trades between clearing members on LIFFE. It is completely independent of LIFFE and owned by six UK clearing banks.

LDCs
Lesser Developed Countries.

Lead Manager
The Institution responsible for putting together a new issue and taking responsibility for its distribution.

Leaver
Client closing his Personal Equity Plan (PEP).

Legacy Currencies
The currencies of the member states participating in Euro. The legacy currencies will eventually disappear and be replaced by Euro.

Lender of Last Resort
A central bank function which provides liquidity to the banking system by lending overnight funds

Letter of Credit
A written undertaking of a bank made at the request of a customer (e.g. importer) to honour the demand for payment from a seller (e.g. exporter) if the terms and conditions of the credit are met.

Level Term Assurance
A policy under which a fixed sum assured will be paid out if the life assured dies during the term of the policy.

Leverage
See *Gearing*.

Liabilities
Amounts owed by a company to suppliers of goods, to bankers and to bondholders.

LIBID
London Interbank Bid Rate – the interest rate at which banks bid (borrow) for cash deposits in the interbank market.

LIBOR
The London Interbank Offered Rate. It is the interest rate used when one bank borrows from another bank and the benchmark used to price many capital market and derivative transactions.

Life Assured
The person whose death will trigger a payment under the terms of a life insurance policy.

LIFFE
The London International Financial Futures and Options Exchange. Market place for trading derivatives on financial instruments, and on soft commodities such as coffee and sugar.

LIMEAN (London Interbank Mean Price)
The average of LIBOR and LIBID.

Limit Order
Type of order input into SETS or an options order in which a buy or a sell price is specified. If not completed immediately the balance is displayed on the screen and forms the Order Book.

Limited Liability
A benefit of share ownership whereby the liability of a shareholder for the debts of a company is limited to the capital subscribed.

Limited Price Indexation (LPI)
The requirement to increase pensions and payments under a final salary scheme by 5% pa or RPI if less.

Liquidation
The formal process of closing down a company. The assets are sold, the liabilities and preference shares are repaid and any balance of assets is paid to the ordinary shareholders.

Liquidity
Ease with which an item can be traded on the market. Liquid markets are described as deep.

Listed Company
Company which has been admitted to listing on a Stock Exchange and whose shares can then be dealt on that Exchange.

Listed Security
A security listed on a major Stock Exchange.

Listing
Status applied for by companies whose securities are then listed on a stock exchange, eg. the London Stock Exchange and available to be traded.

Listing Particulars
Detailed information that must be published by a company applying to be listed.

Listing Rules
Rule book for listed companies which governs their behaviour. Commonly known in the UK as the Yellow Book.

Lloyd's of London
This is the world's largest insurance market, which is sustained by individual members who assume unlimited personal liability for claims. It is exempt from authorisation under the Financial Services Act 1986.

Loan Back
A loan from the life office or other lender under a pension plan.

Loan Stock
Fixed interest stock issued by a company or corporation. Can have a variety of features such as cumulative, preference, redeemable.

Local
An individual member of an exchange who trades solely for his or her own account.

London Code of Conduct
The rules and guidelines drawn up by the Bank of England to regulate and control the activities of the wholesale money markets and foreign exchange markets

London Interbank Bid Rate (LIBID)
See *LIBID*.

London Inter Bank Offer Rate (LIBOR)
See *LIBOR*.

London International Financial Futures and Options Exchange (LIFFE)
See *LIFFE*.

London Metal Exchange (LME)
Market for trading in base metal derivatives such as copper, tin, zinc, etc.

London Stock Exchange (LSE)
Market for trading in securities. Formerly known as the International Stock Exchange of the United Kingdom and Republic of Ireland, the LSE is a Recognised Investment Exchange and as such regulates the

operation of the market place. Additionally, LSE is the UK's Competent Listing Authority and regulates listed companies.

Long
Being the owner of an open bought position.

Long Coupon
A bond on which the first coupon payment period (only) is longer than the normal period.

Long Position
The term used to indicate that an investor or trader holds a quantity of bonds that has not been sold.

Long–dated
Gilts with more than 15 years until redemption.

Longs
Abbreviated name for gilt edged securities with more than 15 years left until final redemption.

Long–Term Care Insurance (LTC)
Insurance taken out to cover the cost of caring for individuals who are unable to perform, say, two or three activities of daily living.

Lot
Alternative term for one option or futures contract.

Low Cost Endowment
Form of endowment policy which combines with a decreasing term assurance. Usually used to provide a low cost method of funding eventual repayment of a mortgage.

Low Cost Whole Life

A low-cost whole of life with-profits policy, in effect combining a with-profits whole life policy with a decreasing term assurance element to provide a guaranteed minimum level of cover.

Low Start Endowment

A low-cost endowment with premiums starting at a low level and rising gradually over a number of years (eg, five years) to the full premium. Normally aimed at house buyers.

M

M0
Narrowest measure of the money supply comprising notes and coins.

M2
Measure of the money supply comprising M0 plus sight deposits.

M4
Measure of the money supply comprising M2 plus all bank and building society deposits.

Maastricht Treaty
The treaty on European Union which amended the Treaty of Rome. The Maastricht Treaty established key criteria which member countries needed to achieve in order to be eligible for EMU.

Making a Price
Market maker offering a selling and buying price for a security (bid and ask prices).

Managed Unit Trust
See *Fund of Funds*.

Managed PEP
May have contained qualifying shares, corporate bonds, unit trusts, investment trusts or combinations of the three. Whilst the manager decided which assets to hold within the pooled investments, the investor often had the choice of selecting the trusts.

Management Buy-Out
The purchase of most or all of a companies share capital by its senior executives or management.

Management Group
The primary group consisting of lead manager, co–lead manager(s) and co–managers, that leads a new issue of bonds.

Manager's Box
See *Book/Box*.

Managing
Buying and selling investments for customers' portfolios either on a discretionary or advisory basis.

Mandatory Quote Period
Time of day during which market makers in equities are obliged to quote prices under London Stock Exchange rules.

Manufactured Dividend
A payment of an amount equal to a dividend payment made by a borrower of securities to a lender of securities, so that the lender receives the coupon amount from the bonds that it would have received had it not lent or repoed out the bonds.

Many-to-Many (MTM)

A CREST transaction type created by dual input complex delivery instructions, through which up to four stock movements and two cash movements can be moved between two participants. It can be used for taking up rights in a rights issue.

Margin

Proportion of the value of futures contracts which must be supplied by both buyers and sellers. It is re-calculated daily.

Mark To Market

The process of revaluing an OTC or exchange-traded product each day. It is the difference between the closing price on the previous day against the current closing price. For exchange-traded products this is referred to as variation margin.

Market

Description of any organisation or facility through which items are traded. All exchanges are markets.

Market Capitalisation

The total value of a company's issued securities at their current market prices. This figure should include all the different types of security issued by the company, but is often used in relationship to the equity market capitalisation.

Market Counterparty

A person dealing as agent or principal with the broker and involved in the same nature of investment business as the broker.

Market Economy

An economic system where individuals have complete freedom to buy and sell whatever goods and services they wish.

Market Forces
Supply and demand allowing buyers and sellers to fix the price without external interference.

Market Maker
A trader who quotes bid and offer prices in the market and is normally under an obligation to make a price at all times.

Market Risk
The risk of financial loss to a portfolio brought about by the movement of market variables.

Master Agreement
This agreement is for OTC transactions and is signed between the client and the broker. It covers the basic terms under which the client and broker wish to transact business. Each individual trade has a separate individual agreement with specific terms known as a confirm.

MATIF
The French International Financial Futures Exchange.

Matching
The process whereby a settlement system compares and attempts to combine settlement instructions in order to achieve an agreed transaction record which can then go on to be settled.

Maturity (Date)
The partial or final repayment of the outstanding debt by the issuer/borrower (on a particular date).

Maximum Investment Plan (MIP)
A unit–linked endowment policy with the minimum sum assured necessary for it to be a qualifying policy.

Medium Dated
Gilts due to be redeemed within the next seven to fifteen years.

Mediums
Abbreviated name for gilt edged securities officially classified as having 8 – 15 years left until final redemption. Most investment advisors consider a gilt with 6–15 years remaining to be a 'medium'.

Memorandum of Association
The document which forms the basis of a companies registration, giving details of its address, powers and objects. See *Articles of Association*.

Merchant Bank
A UK bank which is primarily involved in matters such as portfolio management, bills of exchange acceptance, mergers etc, rather than retail banking business.

Mergers and Acquisitions (M&A)
Divisions of securities houses or merchant banks responsible for advising on takeover activity. Usually work with the corporate finance department and is often kept as a single unit.

Middle (Mid) Price
The price half way between a buying and selling price. This is the price for a share taken at close of the previous days business published in the Financial Times.

MIRAS– Mortgage Interest Relief At Source
The system whereby tax relief on mortgage payments is given by the borrower paying a reduced sum to the lender who claims the shortfall from the Inland Revenue.

Misleading Statement
Giving false information about an investment in order to affect its value.

Mismatch
Where short and long positions do not complement one another.

Mixed economy
Economy which relies on a mix of market forces and government involvement.

Model
A series of mathematical processes that will produce an estimate of the 'fair value' of a financial instrument, eg 'Black Scholes' or the binomial model.

Model Code for Securities Dealing
Part of the Yellow Book that relates to directors dealing in their own company's securities. Prohibits them from doing so during the two months before results are announced.

Money Broker
Formerly, a member firm of the London Stock Exchange authorised to act as an intermediary for stock loans between a market maker who wishes to borrow stock and an authorised institution who has stock to lend. As of January 1996, stock borrowing and lending intermediaries act in this role.

Money Laundering
Process by which criminals attempt to conceal the true origin and ownership of the proceeds of their criminal activities.

Money Laundering Regulations Act 1993
The regulations place the legal obligation on investment houses, etc, in the UK to report suspicious movements of cash. Failure to comply renders the individual liable to a fine and/or imprisonment.

Money Market
A reference to the market where short-term instruments such as certificates of deposit, bankers' acceptances, repurchase agreements are traded. There is no physical market location.

Money Market Fund
A unit trust which invests in deposits and other money market instruments, e.g. Treasury Bills.

Money Purchase Scheme
See *Defined Contribution Scheme.*

Money Purchase Underpin
A minimum benefit eg, capital allowances, provided in a defined benefit scheme, calculated on a money purchase basis.

Money Supply
Measure of the money available in the economy.

Monitoring
Procedure whereby each SRO visits its member firms at regular intervals and checks compliance with the rules.

Monitoring Department
An SFA department responsible for monitoring member firm's compliance and for informing the SFA Investigations Department if it suspects a member firm of misconduct.

Monopolies and Mergers Commission (MMC)
A statutory body that investigates potential monopolies and mergers, monitors privatised industries and watches for anti–competitive practices.

Moody's Investors Services
See *Rating (Credit)*.

Mortgage
Form of secured borrowing. Used mainly in the context of loans taken for the purpose of house purchase.

Mortgage Debenture Stocks
A debenture secured by a fixed charge on the borrower's property assets.

Mutual Funds
An open–ended investment company or trust which combines the contributions of many investors with similar objectives.

Mutual Life Office
Insurance companies which are effectively 'owned' by their with–profits policyholders.

N

Naked Writing/Options
The seller does not own the stock corresponding to the call option which he has sold and would be forced to pay the prevailing market price for the stock to meet delivery obligations, if called.

Names
Individuals of Lloyds of London who join together in syndicates to write insurance business. Their liability is unlimited and therefore all their personal wealth is at risk.

NASDAQ
National Association of Securities Dealers Automated Quotation System is a US screen–based dealing system. It is owned and operated by the National Association of Securities Dealers (NASD) which is an American securities industry self–regulatory organisation. Companies listed on NASDAQ are often smaller, newer companies, especially in the higher technology sector.

National Association of Pension Funds (NAPF)
Trade association of pension funds through which they can voice their opinions collectively.

Nostro
Italian word for "our", usually associated with accounts maintained by banks held with other banks in another currency and country. See *Vostro*.

Notice of Cancellation
In circumstances where the right to cancel exists, this document, which explains those rights must be sent within 14 days of the agreement.

Notice of Investigation
Served by the SFA Investigations Department on a person prior to an investigation. Sets out details of the suspected misconduct concerned.

Novation
The process where registered trades are cancelled with the clearing members and substituted by two new ones – one between the clearing house and the clearing member seller, the other between the clearing house and the clearing member buyer.

NYSE
See *New York Stock Exchange*.

National Central Securities Depository (NCSD)
A CSD which deals specifically with (and is usually based in the country of) domestic instruments eg. CREST for the UK and Ireland.

National Criminal Intelligence Service (NCIS)
Organisation to whom suspicions of money laundering are reported.

National Insurance Contributions (NICS)
A form of tax theoretically used to fund the social security system although in fact there is no link between the amounts received and amounts paid. The payment structure is split into Classes with differing amounts paid by employees, their employers and the self-employed.

National Savings
Government department which provides savings products to the public with the objective of raising funds for the government. Most transactions are conducted through main branches of post offices.

National Savings Stock Register (NSSR)
Selection of gilts purchasable through Post Offices at very low commission. Income tax is not deducted at source from dividends.

National Securities Clearing Corporation (NSCC)
An organisation providing settlement and clearing facilities in the USA.

Nationality Declaration
A statement of compliance from a purchaser of shares in a company whose Memorandum and Articles of Association specify a limit to shareholders who are not of specified nationality.

Near Cash
Assets which may be converted into cash very quickly, e.g. Treasury Bills and certificates of deposit.

Nearby Month
The first available month for derivatives trading.

Net Asset Value (NAV)
This is the value of the underlying shares held in the portfolio based on quoted mid-market prices, together with other assets, less liabilities, divided by the number of shares in issue. NAV is quoted in pence per share.

Net Income Yield
The income return on an investment after tax has been deducted.

Net Present Value (NPV)
The economic value of a known set of future cash flows calculated by discounting the cash flows at the rates applicable to the future periods to produce a present value for each cash flow

Net Redemption Yield (NRY)
After tax equivalent of the Gross Redemption Yield. This is the measure which should be used by taxpayers in selecting the gilt in which to invest.

Net Relevant Earnings (NRE)
Self–employed earnings or earnings from a non–pensionable employment less certain deductions. NRE is used to determine the maximum contributions to a retirement annuity or personal pension plan. See *Earnings Cap*.

New Issues
Issue of shares arising from the flotation of a company on the stockmarket.

New York Stock Exchange (NYSE)
The NYSE is the world's largest stock exchange. Dealing takes place on the floor of the Exchange or through a computer system called SuperDot.

Nikkei Dow Index
Main share index in Japan.

Nil Paid Shares
New shares offered to existing shareholders by way of a rights issue can normally be bought and sold in a nil paid form up to a week before the call is due. The price is usually, but not necessarily, the difference between the call price and the price of existing shares. (See Rights Issue and Fully Paid Shares).

Nominal
The quantity or amount of securities irrespective of its market value.

Nominal Rate Of Interest
Actual rate of interest paid which comprises the real rate plus inflation. See *Real Rate of Interest*.

Nominal Value (or par value)
The face value of a share as against its market value. For example, a company may have an issued capital of £10 million, divided into 40 million shares of 25p. Par values may be of any amount. They have no real significance, being purely a matter of law and book keeping.

Nominated Advisor
Firm appointed to advise AIM company directors on their responsibilities. Role can be combined with that of nominated broker.

Nominated Broker
Firm appointed to assist dealing in AIM securities.

Nominee
Legal arrangement whereby securities are held by a third party on behalf of the beneficial owner. For administrative reasons, securities are more than likely to be held in a nominee name.

Nominee Company
A company set up to hold shares on behalf of other companies or individuals. Used by custodians and stockbrokers to hold shares on behalf of their customers or clients.

Non-Certificated Shares
Shares for which no certificate is issued to the unit holder.

Non-Clearing Member
A member of an exchange who does not undertake to settle their business. This type of member must appoint a clearing member to register all their trades at the clearing organisation.

Non-Contributory Pension Scheme
Occupational Scheme funded entirely by the employer.

Non-Cumulative Preference Share
If the company fails to pay a preference dividend the entitlement to the dividend is simply lost. There is no accumulation.

Non-Discretionary Dealing
Client takes decisions to buy/sell investments.

Non-Discretionary Securities Lending
A form of securities lending where the custodian seeks approval for each loan from its client on a case-by-case basis.

Non-Fungible
Securities which have the same security code and which are identifiable by separate certificate numbers. These securities are not interchangeable. See *Fungible*.

Non-Private Customers
Those customers who the rules do not require firms to classify as private and therefore to whom limited duties of protection are owed.

Non-Profit Insurance
A policy which does not participate in the profits of the life office. A non-profit whole of life policy pays out only a fixed sum assured whenever death occurs. A non-profit endowment policy pays out a fixed sum assured on maturity or earlier death. Most term assurance policies are non-profit policies.

Non-Qualifying
With respect to unit trusts or investment trusts where more than 50% of the underlying comprise shares in companies, regardless of where incorporated, which are quoted on a recognised stock exchange. A maximum of £1,500 of the annual allowance may be invested in such funds.

Non-Qualifying Policy
A policy that does not qualify for full tax relief and where the proceeds on maturity, surrender or death may be subject to higher rate tax.

No Par Value (NPV)
Shares which do not possess a nominal or par value. Such a method of not expressing a par value is not allowed in the UK where securities must be given a nominal value. In the US however, the issue of shares of no par value is quite common and from time to time the matter is debated in this country. One problem with par value is that special rules apply to the raising of new money when existing securities stand at a discount on par value, which makes the raising of new money difficult in such circumstances.

Normal Bonus
Also known as a reversionary bonus. The bonus added each year to a with profits policy. Once declared this bonus cannot be withdrawn.

Normal Market Size (NMS)
Minimum size in which market makers must quote on LSE.

O

OAT
French government bond issued with a maturity between 7 and 30 years.
Also an Own Account Transfer in CREST/CGO – a transfer of stock between two accounts under the same CREST/CGO participant.

Occupational Pension Scheme
Pension scheme run by an individual employer for the benefit of its employees. Could be contributory or non–contributory. Maximum pension payable is limited by Inland Revenue rules.

Occupational Pensions Board (OPB)
A statutory body responsible for issuing contracting out and appropriate scheme certificates for pension schemes which meet the statutory requirements. The OPB supervises schemes to ensure that GMPs and protected rights are secure and ensures that equal access and preservation requirements are satisfied.

OEICs
Open–Ended Investment Companies (pronounced OIKs). New corporate structure introduced in 1997. It is a form of collective investment vehicle. Its share capital can expand or contract.

Off Balance Sheet Transaction
A transaction which affects the assets or liabilities or an organisation, but is not required by accounting standards to be reported as such.

Offer
The rate at which the market or a dealer is willing to sell.

Offer Basis
Circumstances where the trust manager has set the offer price of an authorised unit trust at the highest level allowed by FSA rules.

Offer For Sale
Method for a company to issue shares and come to the market for the first time. Anyone can apply for shares through the publicly available application forms.

Offer Price
See *Ask Price*.

Offer–to–Bid
Performance comparison unique to the unit trust industry.

Offer–to–Bid Basis
The usual form of unit trust performance appraisal – the opening price used for the calculation is the then current offer price and the closing price is the then current bid price.

Off-the-page advertisement
Advertisements which appear in the press and which contain application forms for purchasing units. If used the investor does not have rights to cancel the investment.

Office of Fair Trading (OFT)
Government department which administers the Fair Trading legislation and advises the Secretary of State for Trade and Industry on whether or not a proposed takeover should be referred to the MMC for full investigation.

Offshore Investment
Any investment made by an individual who is resident or domiciled in one country, into an investment medium based in another country. An investment centre which is offshore is not subject to UK tax or regulations.

Omnibus Account
See *Pooled Nominee Account*.

One sided confirmation
Only one party to the transaction, usually the broker or dealer, submits trade details to a centralised trade confirmation system. The other counterparty merely affirms or rejects the trade.

On–exchange/Off–exchange
Any transactions conducted on a RIE or a DIE are termed 'on–exchange', whereas those on any other market are known as 'off–exchange'. The latter are subject to special reporting Financial Services Authority/SRO rules.

Open Economy
A country where there are few restrictions on trading with other countries.

Open Ended
Type of organisation such as Unit Trusts or OEICs which can expand without limit. Where the total of units on offer can rise or fall according to customer demand.

Open Ended Investment Companies (OEICs)
See *OEICs*.

Open Interest
The number of contracts outstanding with the market in a particular instrument.

Open Market Option
The right to take the accumulated fund from a personal pension scheme or retirement annuity plan in order to purchase an annuity from another life office.

Open Offer
This is an offer to existing shareholders to subscribe money to buy further shares, usually at a discount to the market price. Although set out on a pro rata basis, shareholders may subscribe for any amount of shares.

Open Outcry
The style of trading whereby traders face each other in a designated area such as a pit and shout or call their respective bids and offers. Hand signals are also used to communicate. It is governed by exchange rules.

Open Position
A position held with a clearing house (or other counterparty) or a trade that has not been counteracted by an equal and opposite trade.

Opening
Undertaking a transaction which creates a position.

Opening Trade
A bought or sold trade which is held open to create a position.

Operational Risk
The risk to an organisation of failures in the systems, procedures and routines in the dealing support areas.

Option
An option gives the holder the right (but not the obligation) to buy or sell a fixed quantity of an underlying asset on or before a specified date in the future. There are two basic types of traded option – puts and calls. The buyer of a call option has the right to buy the underlying asset at a given price. The seller (also known as the writer) has the obligation to sell shares to him, if the option is exercised. Conversely, the buyer of a put option has the right to sell the underlying asset at the given price. The writer of a put option is obliged to buy stock from the holder if the option is exercised.

Option Premium
The sum of money paid by the buyer, for acquiring the right of the option. It is the sum of money received by the seller for incurring the obligation, having sold the rights, of the option. It is the sum of the intrinsic value and the time value.

Options On Futures
These have the same characteristics as an option, the difference being that the underlying product is either a long or short futures contract. Premium is not exchanged as the contracts are marked to market each day.

Order Book
See *Stock Exchange Electronic Trading System (SETS)*.

Order driven
Dealing system in which prices are determined by the direct flow of buying and selling orders.

Ordinary Business Investor
Customer of an investment business which is a business entity and which meets the size criteria such that it does not have to be given the same levels of protection as a private customer.

Ordinary Shares
Shares which are the risk capital of the company. These shares carry no guarantees and reflect the success (or failure) of the company. The ordinary shareholders are the true owners of the company who are entitled to the balance of the income of the company after all expenses have been paid.

OTC
See *Over the Counter*.

Out-Of-The-Money
A call option whose exercise price is above the current underlying share price or a put option whose exercise price is below the current underlying share price. This option has no intrinsic value.

Outright
Simple foreign exchange transaction involving the purchase of one currency for another at a specific exchange rate.

Out-Trade
A trade which has been incorrectly matched on the floor of an exchange. These types of trades should normally be resolved by the end of the business day on which they were traded.

Overdraft
A loan on individuals current/banking accounts which enables them to withdraw extra funds up to an agreed limit and for a specific period of time.

Over The Counter (OTC)
Generic name for trading in any product outside a formal exchange. In contrast to exchange traded products which are standardised but offer greater liquidity.

Oversubscribed
Applications have been received for more shares than are available in a new issue.

Over-The-Bridge
The electronic link between Euroclear and Cedel which allows book entry movements of securities between customers of either clearing house.

Overnight Indexed Swaps (OIS)
A tool for managing short term interest rate risk.

P

Packaged Products
Life assurance, pensions and unit trusts.

Paid In Surplus
See *Share Premium Account*.

Paid-Up Benefit
A preserved benefit which is secured for an individual member under an insurance policy where the premiums have stopped being paid for the member.

Paid-Up Policy (PUP)
A policy that was a regular premium policy but has been converted to a PUP at the policyholder's request. No further premiums are paid and the benefits previously guaranteed are accordingly reduced.

Panel on Takeovers and Mergers (POTOM)
A non-statutory body comprising City institutions which regulates takeover activities.

Paper Interface
The mechanics by which investors who have certificated holdings settle transactions, once the company has become a CREST participant. It also includes the way in which CREST members convert certificated holdings into dematerialised holdings (ie, stock deposit). See *CREST Courier and Sorting Service*.

Par Value
See *Nominal Value*.

Pari passu
Equal in all respects (Latin). A corporate action in which a line of stock is issued by a company which is identical to the existing class of security (except perhaps that it does not qualify for the dividend or has some other restriction).

Partly Paid Bonds
Bonds in which a proportion of the price is not due immediately payable, but falls due on a fixed date in the future.

Partnership Insurance
An insurance policy which pays out on the death of a partner, normally allowing the survivors to buy the deceased partner's interest in the business.

Part–withdrawal
A withdrawal of cash or securities from a Personal Equity Plan account. A written instruction from the plan holder is required in order to release the funds.

Party Transaction Status
The transaction status which reflects the input status of one party to a transaction type, designed to reflect the logical stage in a member's input. Sometimes referred to as 'party status'.

Passive Investment Management
Investment management which is not seeking to outperform the market, but only looking for a fair return for the risk involved, ie, the market average return.

Pay Date
In a benefit distribution, the date on which the benefit is distributed by an issuer.

Paying Agent
The financial institution appointed by the borrower and responsible for making due interest payments and principal repayments to bondholders against presentation of the coupon or bond certificate.

Payment Bank
A CREST participant who is obliged by contract with each CREST member, each payment bank and CREST to guarantee payment for securities delivered to their customers through CREST. Settlement of these obligations takes place outside CREST although the system creates and records the obligations.

Payment versus Payment (PvP)
The simultaneous payment and receipt of the currencies involved in a foreign exchange deal.

Penny Share
A low priced and often speculative share.

Pension Fund
Provider of pensions. Status requires Inland Revenue approval and means that the organisation does not pay any tax.

Pensioners' Bond
National Savings Product exclusively available to those aged 60 or over. A lump sum investment is made which then provides a monthly income.

PEP (Personal Equity Plan)
See *Personal Equity Plan*.

PEPable Investments
Securities which may be held in a PEP.

Periodic Charge
See *Annual Management Charge*.

Permanent Health Insurance (PHI)
Policies designed to replace income in the event of the policyholder being unable to work due to illness.

Permanent Interest Bearing Shares (PIBS)
Permanent Interest–Bearing Shares are issued by building societies and pay a fixed rate of interest for an indefinite period (they are irredeemable). PIBS repayment rank behind all other creditors for capital.

Permitted Person
Someone who has applied to the Financial Services Authority under Paragraph 23 of Financial Services Authority rules for permission to carry out deals in the course of non–investment business (eg, treasury department of conglomerate).

Perpetual Bond
A bond which has no maturity date.

Personal Account Dealing
Transactions conducted by employees for their own account and not for a customer or for their employer.

Personal Account Notice
A written summary given to all member firm employees detailing the rules on own account dealings.

Personal Allowances
The amount of annual income that each person is allowed to earn which is not liable to income tax. The amount differs according to whether a person is married or single and according to age.

Personal Equity Plan (PEP)
An investment plan managed by a plan manager, approved by the Revenue, and managed in accordance with PEP regulations. No additional PEPs may be taken out after April 1999.

Personal Identification Number (PIN)
A unique numerical number which is keyed into a computer machine to gain access eg. ATM.

Personal Investment Authority (PIA)
The SRO with responsibility for regulating firms advising on and arranging deals in life assurance and personal pensions, friendly society investments, unit trusts and investment trust savings schemes.

Personal Pension Plan (PPP)
An Inland Revenue approved scheme under which individuals who are self–employed or in non-pensionable employment can make pension contributions for retirement and/or life assurance benefits. Employers can also contribute to PPPs.

Personal Pensions
Pension schemes taken out by an individual to provide funds for his or her retirement. Are essential for the self-employed and can also be used by employees not in an occupational scheme. Payments into the scheme are limited by Inland Revenue rules.

Physical Delivery
Delivery of definitive or material certificates in a security. More commonly, ownership of securities is transferred by book entry transfer. Also applies to deliveries of underlying commodities in an options or futures contract.

Physical Securities
Securities represented in the form of certificates.

PIA
See *Personal Investment Authority*.

PIN
See *Personal Identification Number*.

Pit
The designated area on the market floor where a particular contract is traded. It may be termed a ring in some markets, e.g., LME.

Placing
Procedure used for new issues where a securities house contacts its own clients to offer them stock.

Plain Vanilla or Vanilla Swap
A swap which has a very basic structure.

PLC
Public Limited Company (UK).

Polarisation
FSA requirement whereby firms selling long term financial products must either act as a company representative and only sell that one company's products or act as an independent financial adviser and recommend from all companies' products.

Policy Protection Board
Organisation established under the Policyholders Protection Act 1975 to ensure compensation and continuity of cover for holders of long term insurance products.

Pooled Nominee Account
Investors' securities are registered in the name of the nominee. The details of the beneficial owners are maintained in the records of the nominee rather than the records of the issuer's registrar.

Portfolio
Collection of financial assets which is designed to achieve a specific investment objective.

Portfolio Balance Model
The theory of exchange rate determination which concentrates on the analysis of capital investment flows.

Position
The quantity of bonds held by an investor. See *Long and Short Positions*.

POTOM
See *Panel on Takeovers and Mergers*.

Potential Future Exposure
The risk of an increase in credit exposure due to a movement in external market conditions

Pound Cost Averaging
A feature of the regular investment of a fixed sum. Because the fixed sum buys more units when the price is lower and fewer when it is higher, the effect is to make the average price paid for the units bought more advantageous than investing a lump sum at one time.

Pre–emption Right
The right of a shareholder whereby a company making a new issue of shares must offer the shares to the existing shareholders in proportion to their existing holdings. Also called a rights issue.

Preference Shares
Shares which carry rights to a fixed amount of dividend and return of capital in priority to ordinary shares.

Premium
The price that an option buyer pays and a writer receives when trading an option.

Preserved Benefits
The benefits payable at a later date when an individual stops being an active member of a pension scheme. Preserved pensions from a final salary occupational scheme relating to service since 1 January 1985 generally have to be increased by RPI or 5% per annum whichever is the lower (limited price indexation – LPI). LPI applies for all preserved benefits for those who left a scheme on or after 1 January 1991.

Price
The cash amount payable or receivable per minimum nominal amount of a security.

Price/Earnings Ratio (PER)
Measure of how a company is rated by the stock market. A high ratio implies that the company is well thought of for its future prospects and vice versa. Calculated by dividing the share price by the company's latest year's earnings per share.

Primary Dealer
See *Gilt Edged Market Maker*.

Primary Issue
An issue of new shares when a company is first admitted to an Exchange.

Primary Market
Initial launch of a company's shares when they first become available for a trading on the Stock Market.

Principal
The nominal amount of a bond due to be repaid at maturity.

Principal Trading
When a member firm of the London Stock Exchange buys stock from or sells stock to a non-member for its own account, ie. not as an agent.

Principal-To-Principal Market
A market where the clearing house only recognises the clearing member as one entity, and not the underlying clients of the clearing member.

Private Customer
Classification of those customers who are financially unsophisticated and require most protection within the rules. FSA 1986 was primarily designed for the benefit of private customers.

Private Investor
An individual who holds shares solely for their own benefit.

Private Medical Insurance (PMI)
Also known as medical expenses insurance, it provides cover for private medical treatment.

Privatisation
Process whereby the government puts state owned industries into the private sector, eg, water, electricity. Usually involves an offer for sale of its shares.

Probate/Confirmation
Legal document nominating executors and detailing total value of the estate.

Product Particulars
Factual information about the investment, which must accompany notices of the right to cancel. The purpose is to ensure that the investor knows what he or she is acquiring. Details include the investment objectives, dealing procedures, charges, the yield, dealing spread and the name of the trustee.

Profit and Loss Account
Financial statement showing how the profit of the company has arisen over a period of time, usually a year, leading up to the balance sheet date. Under US reporting, the profit and loss account is called the income statement.

Profit Sharing Scheme
Profits of a company given to their employees in the form of shares. Employees may be given share options where they can purchase shares at a fixed price or they may be able to buy shares under a save–as–you–earn scheme.

Project A
The after-hours trading system used by the Chicago Board of Trade.

Program Trade
One of a number of trading strategies which involve the simultaneous purchase or sale of a number of different shares.

Property Bond
Single premium insurance policy where the funds are invested in property.

Proposal Form
Form used to apply for a life policy.

Proprietary Trader
A trader who deals as a principal for an organisation such as an investment bank taking advantage of short-term price movements as well as taking long-term views on whether the market will move up or down.

Proprietary Office
Life offices that are owned by shareholders. If the life office runs a with-profits fund, the shareholders and with-profits policy holders share the profits: normally 10% to shareholders and 90% to policyholders.

Prospectus
See *Listing Particulars*.

Protected Rights
The benefits under an Appropriate Personal Pension Scheme from the contributions paid by the DSS for a member who has contracted out of SERPS. Also the benefits secured from the minimum payments than must be made to contract an employee out of SERPS.

Proxy
A person appointee by a shareholder to vote on their behalf at company meetings.

Proxy Voting
Voting on company issues by a representative (the proxy) of the shareholder.

PTM Levy
A flat-rate levy on agency bargains which is collected to finance the Panel on Takeovers and Mergers (POTOM).

Public Offer
An offer to sell shares to the public, usually on the flotation of a company on the stock market.

Public Sector
Areas of the economy which are owned by central and local government.

Public Sector Borrowing Requirement (PSBR)
See *Public Sector Net Cash Requirement*.

Public Sector Net Cash Requirement (PSNCR)
If the government spends more than it receives from tax and other revenues, the shortfall is known as the Public Sector Net Cash Requirement. This shortfall was until June 1998 known as the Public Sector Borrowing Requirement (PSBR).

Purchase Fund
A fund set aside by the borrower and used to repurchase a specified amount of its bonds at or below a specified price.

Purchasing Power Parity (PPP)
A theory for the determination of exchange rates based upon the relative value of a basket of internationally traded goods and services in different countries.

Pure Endowment
A policy which pays out only if the life assured lives until the maturity date.

Put
A bondholder's right to sell the bonds back to the borrower in accordance with pre-agreed terms.

Put Option
Provides the buyer (holder) of the option with the right to sell the underlying instrument at the agreed price.

Q

Qualifying Policy
A life assurance policy which meets rules set out in Taxes Act 1988. Qualifying policies taken out before 14 March 1984 may qualify for life assurance premium relief (LAPR). Policy proceeds on death or maturity are free of personal tax.

Quote Driven
Dealing system where some firms accept the responsibility to quote buying and selling prices, moving these prices to stimulate business.

Quoted
Colloquial term for a security that is traded on the Stock Exchange.

Quoted Currency
The currency in a foreign exchange deal the amount of which is equated to one unit of the 'base currency'.

R

Rating (Credit)
An indication of the credit quality of a bond. The ratings are prepared and updated by independent agencies such as Moody's Investors Services and Standard & Poor's.

RCH
Recognised Clearing House under the Financial Services Act (FSA).

Real Rate Of Interest
Amount by which the nominal rate of interest exceeds inflation. See *Nominal Rate of Interest*.

Real Time
Indices of some stock market prices are said to be calculated in real time. Data is fed into a computer and a new share price index is calculated as soon as changes occur.

Realised Profit
Profit which has arisen from an actual sale or other disposal of assets.

Real Time Gross Settlement (RTGS)
The settlement mechanism of a payment system involving the movement of funds between accounts over the books of the central bank in real time.

Rebate–Only Personal Pension
An Appropriate Personal Pension Scheme funded solely by rebates of National Insurance contributions (and tax relief and additional payments/incentives) paid by the DSS to a pension provider for an employee contracted out of SERPS.

Receiver
Person appointed to wind up a company.

Receiving Agent
An organisation appointed by a company to assist it in administering a corporate action, for example, a takeover or a rights issue by receiving acceptances/applications from investors.

Recognised Collective Investment Schemes
Non UK–based unit trusts which FSA has recognised as being adequately regulated and which can be marketed freely in the UK, subject to adherence with UK marketing standards.

Recognised Investment Exchange (RIE)
Status granted by FSA to UK exchanges which it believes are acceptable in the quality of market services they provide.

Recognised Professional Body (RPB)
Organisation recognised by the Financial Services Authority, which controls a profession whose members have ancillary involvement in investment business eg. ICAEW.

Recognised Stock Exchange
A Stock Exchange approved by the Inland Revenue under the Taxes Act.

Reconciliation
Matching of stock held in safe custody against client portfolio records and other comparisons.

Record Date
This date, set by the company, determines those shareholders who are entitled to receive a specific benefit on their shareholding. This may include dividends, rights or in some instances, incentives.

Recovery Stock
Shares in a company whose profits have fallen substantially but are expected to recover in the future.

Redemption
The repayment of the principal amount of a bond by the borrower.

Redemption Date
The date on which the borrower will repay the capital on a loan stock or the government will repay the capital on a gilt.

Redemption Yield
The total annualised return on owning a fixed interest security, made up of annual income plus any gain or minus any loss to redemption.

Referral
The Secretary of State for Trade and Industry refers a proposed takeover to the Monopolies and Mergers Commission (MMC) who then investigates further.

Regional Custody
A term used to describe the custody of securities traded within a geographical region, e.g. European countries only or Far Eastern countries only.

Register
The legal record of company shareholders.

Register Update Request (RUR)
An instruction generated by CREST for a registrar, requesting that the register be changed to reflect a movement of stock between member accounts in CREST.

Registered Securities
Shares or bonds whose ownership is recorded on a central register as opposed to bearer securities.

Registered Title
Form of ownership of securities where the owner's name appears on a register maintained by the company.

Registrar
A quoted company usually appoints a registrar to manage its shareholder records. This company is responsible for the administration of the share register, distributing shareholder information on behalf of the company and paying dividends to shareholders.

Registrar of Companies
Government official whose department is responsible for keeping records of all companies.

Regular Income Plans
The use of several income–oriented unit trusts to provide an investor with either a monthly or quarterly income.

Regular Member
A type of broker on the Tokyo Stock Exchange.

Regular Premium
Policies where the premiums are paid at regular intervals, usually monthly.

Regulated Unit Trusts
Those trusts which can be freely marketed in the UK. Any trusts based in the UK would be authorised by FSA and overseas trusts would have to be recognised by them.

Renewable Term Assurance
Type of term assurance where the policy is renewable at the end of its original term without further medical examination.

Renewal Commission
A fee (typically 0.5%) paid to IFAs, usually on an annual basis, out of the fund manager's charge. It is paid on funds which remain in the unit trust. The purpose is to encourage long term investment and remunerate the IFA for servicing the client. Also known as trail commission.

Renunciation Form
The form which may appear on the back of a unit trust certificate or may be separate and which the holder(s) signs when selling units back to the managers. The form is the formal transfer of legal title to the managers of the units being redeemed.

Repayment Mortgage
Form of mortgage where the monthly payments made are a combination of interest and capital.

Repo (Sale and repurchase)
Transaction in gilts, where the gilt is sold with a price and date fixed for its re-purchase. UK government allowed gilts to be traded on the repo market in 1996. Repos can also be transacted for Bonds and Equities.

Reportable Transactions
Any product traded off-exchange by a member firm.

Reporting Risk
The risk of decisions being taken on the basis of incorrect, incomplete or badly specified reports.

Repurchase Agreement (Repo)
See *Repo*.

Residual Settlement
Settlement which takes place outside CREST. If both the transferee and transferor are CREST members, CREST can facilitate residual settlement using the CCSS and CREST payment instructions.

Resolution
A proposal put to shareholders at a general meeting.

Retail Price Index (RPI)
Monthly Index that shows the movement of retail prices in the UK.

Retained Benefits
Retirement or death benefits due to an employee from a previous period of employment or self-employment. These may have to be taken into account in calculating maximum approvable benefits under an occupational scheme.

Retirement Annuity Plan (RAP)
Also known as Section 226 or RAC. Contracts issued on or before 30 June 1988 for self–employed people and employees with non–pensionable earnings. Maximum pension contributions are based on net relevant earnings. RAPs are not subject to the pension cap, but lower percentage contribution limits apply.

Reuters
A news agency that provides instant access to bond and equity prices and news information via monitors located in subscribers' offices. There are some 100,000 subscribers in 120 countries.

Reverse
The opposite stance of a counterparty to a Repo Agreement. The reverse is a purchase of bonds with the simultaneous sale back to the repo counterparty for future settlement.

Reverse Repo
Purchase of gilt where the price and date for its re–sale is fixed at the same time.

Reversionary Bonus
See *Normal Bonus*.

Revocable Payment
A payment instruction that can be cancelled unilaterally by the sender.

RIE
See *Recognised Investment Exchange*.

Right Of Offset
Where positions and cash held by the Clearing Organisation in different accounts for a member are allowed to be netted.

Rights Issue
Rights issues are capital raising exercises by companies in which existing shareholders are given the right to buy the new shares normally at a discount to the market price for the existing shares.

Ring
The designated area on the market floor where a particular contract is traded. It may be termed a pit in some markets, e.g. LIFFE.

Risk
Risk is best defined as the degree of exposure to change of a portfolio. This may be exposure to a change in the market (known as market risk) or to movement in a specific stock (specific risk). Systemic risk is defined as exposure to the stability of the financial system. There are also risks associated with currency and interest rate exposure.

Risk, counterparty
Risk of non–fulfilment of a trade contract due to inability or unwillingness of the counterparty to complete the transaction.

Risk, operational
Risk of loss due to clerical errors, organisational deficiency, delays, fraud, system failure, non–performance by third party providers and similar events.

Risk, settlement
Risk that a party will default on one or more delivery or payment obligations to its counterparty or to a settlement agent.

Risk, systemic
The risk that the inability of one institution to meet its obligations when due will cause a large number of other participants or financial firms to be unable to meet their obligations when due (chain reaction).

Risk Warning
Document outlining the risks that must be dispatched and signed by private customers before they deal in derivatives.

Roll Over
Transferring a position from one delivery month to another, usually closing the nearby month to open a position in a far month.

Rolling Settlement
System whereby bargains are settled a set number of days after being transacted.

Rotation
The process by which all series of options on an underlying stock are sequentially quoted. On LIFFE all series are rotated at the opening and at the close of business, but a rotation may be requested at any other time.

Round Trip
An opening transaction and its corresponding closing trade are known as a round trip. Dealing charges are sometimes quoted on a round trip basis.

RTGS
Real Time Gross Settlement system, an interbank system to eliminate interbank risk during the day.

Running Yield
See *Flat Yield*.

Running a Book
Firms which are buying and selling stock for themselves hoping to profit from price differences are said to run a book in that stock.

S

Saitori
A member of the Tokyo Stock Exchange who acts as an intermediary between brokers.

Sale of rights nil paid
The sale of the entitlement to take up a rights issue.

Same Day Settlement
A transaction where trade execution and settlement take place on the same day.

Samurai Bonds
A Yen bond issued in Japan by a non–Japanese issuer.

Savings Plan
Schemes run by unit trust groups enabling investors to purchase units conveniently on a regular, usually monthly, basis. Similar schemes are offered by some Investment Trusts.

SAYE (Save As You Earn Employee Share Scheme)
A scheme which qualifies for treatment under the provisions of the Income & Corporation Taxes Act 1988 enabling employees to acquire shares in the company for which they work with advantageous tax treatment and at a special price.

SBLI
Stock Borrowing and Lending Intermediary.

Scaling Down
When applying for shares in a company joining the stock market (see *New Issues*), investors may only receive a proportion of their application if there is an oversubscription and a refund cheque will be sent.

Scheme Particulars
A detailed document which must be available for every authorised or recognised unit trust, giving full particulars of the fund and how it operates.

Screen–Based Trading
A method of trading which takes place by the dealers inputting their bids and offers into screens linked to a computer system. There is no exchange floor and the traders operate the computer screens from their own offices.

Scrip Dividends
To enable a company to save tax, it may offer its shareholders shares instead of a cash dividend.

Scrip Issue
See *Bonus Issue*.

SDRN
See *Stock Deposit Reference Number*.

SDRT
See *Stamp Duty Reserve Tax*.

SEAQ
See *Stock Exchange Automated Quotations System*.

Seasoned Bonds
Bonds that have been traded in the secondary markets for some time (90 days for eurobonds).

Seat
The term given to describe the membership of an exchange which entitles the holder to execute business on the exchange and in certain cases carries voting rights. A seat must be held in order to be a member of an exchange and they can be purchased from the exchange or can be leased from other member firms, depending upon availability.

SEATS Plus
An order–driven system used on the London Stock Exchange for securities which do not attract at least two firms of market makers and also used for all AIM securities.

SEC
See *Securities and Exchange Commission*.

Second Section
The second tier market of the Tokyo Stock Exchange.

Secondary Issue
An issue of new shares by a company which is already listed; examples are rights issues and scrip issues.

Secondary Market
Market place for trading in existing securities. The price at which they are trading has no direct effect on the company's fortunes but is a reflection of investors' perceptions of the company.

Section 32 Policy
Schemes provided by insurance companies to receive transfer values to replace a member's entitlement to pension scheme benefits, normally when a member's pensionable service ends. Sometimes known as buy–out bonds.

Section 47
See *Misleading Statements*.

Section 62
See *Action for Damages*.

Secured Bond
A bond where the company has pledged assets to back the bond. In the event of default the assets are then available to repay the bond.

Securities
Tradeable financial instruments such as, for example, equities and bonds.

Securities and Exchange Commission (SEC)
The overall stock exchange regulatory body for the USA.

Securities and Futures Authority Limited (SFA)
The Self Regulating Organisation (SRO) for dealers in securities, financial and commodity derivatives and corporate financiers. Its responsibilities will be taken over by the FSA.

Securities Institute
The UK professional body for qualified and experienced practitioners engaged in a wide range of securities and other financial services businesses.

Securities and Investments Board (SIB)
Former name of the Financial Services Authority.

Securities Borrowing
A method by which market makers and other firms acting as principals are able to borrow securities in order to make up a shortage in those securities and in exchange for a fee.

Securities House
General term covering any type of organisation involved in securities although usually reserved for the larger firms.

Securities Lending
Authorised institutions lend their assets and, when permitted, those of their clients to market makers through a network of intermediaries in exchange for a fee.

Segmentation
Use of a cluster of small identical policies rather than a large one.

Segregation
See *Designated Nominee Account*.

Segregation of Funds
Where the client assets are held separately from those assets belonging to the member firm.

Selective Marketing
See *Placing*.

Self Regulating Organisations (SROs)
Bodies which receive their status from FSA and are able to regulate sectors of the financial services industry. Regulation by an SRO provides authorisation. Will be phased out under the new financial services legislation.

Self–Administered Scheme
A scheme where the assets are invested by the trustees usually with the assistance of investment managers, instead of purchasing insurance policies.

Self–Invested Personal Pension (SIPP)
A personal pension under which the member can control the investments and invest in eg, unit trusts, stocks and shares.

Selling Price
Price at which units are sold, inclusive of the initial and compulsory charges.

Sell–Out
A mechanism which, in the case of non–receipt of the bonds by the buyer, gives a seller the chance to deliver the bonds by selling the bonds to another counterparty. The original deal is subsequently closed out.

Senior Debt
Debt which ranks above other unsecured or subordinated debt in the event of the borrower's default.

Sensitivity
The amount by which the value of a portfolio is vulnerable or sensitive to changes in interest rates.

SEQUAL
The checking system used in the UK for international equities.

Series
All option contracts on the same underlying stock with the same exercise price, expiry price and contract size belong to the same series.

SERPS
The State Earnings Related Pension Scheme which pays a pension according to the level of a person's earnings. Many companies contract out.

SETS
See *Stock Exchange Electronic Trading System*.

Settlement
The fulfilment of the contractual commitments such as payment of cash for securities: the conclusion of a securities transaction by delivery.

Settlement, Fixed
The pre-determined date(s) in a month when transactions are due to settle.

Settlement, Rolling
Settlement takes place on a certain number of days after the trade date. e.g. Eurobond trades settle on the 3rd business day after trade (T+3). Shares in the UK normally trade T+5 or T+10.

Settlement/Settlement Day
There are two types of settlement: rolling settlement and cash settlement. New shares resulting from rights issues or new issues are usually dealt for cash. Settlement is on the business day following the business day of dealing. With rolling settlement, it is the day on which settlement is due for both purchase and sale transactions via the Stock Exchange. In the UK this is currently T+5 (Trade plus 5 working days), but there are suggestions to reduce this to T+3.

Settlement Date
The date on which a transaction is contractually due to settle. Bonds settle on a certain set number of days after the trade date (a rolling basis), eg, eurobonds settle on the 3rd business day after trade (T+3). In some cases, there are bonds which settle on a fixed date during a month.

Settlement Due Date
Intended settlement date – the earliest date a transaction can settle, as indicated in the mandatory and matchable field on settlement instructions for dual input transactions.

Settlement Instruction
The mechanism within CREST for moving stock and/or money between participants whereby each counterparty transmits a settlement instruction to CREST, via the network, for matching. A generic settlement instruction is used by all participants, regardless of their role in the market; the type of transaction is indicated by entry of the three–character transaction type. CREST does not accept pre–matched instructions from other matching or trade confirmation systems.

Settlement Money
Money held under IMRO or PIA rules which has been paid by a client or a firm in respect of securities bought, but for which payment is not yet due. It must be kept separate from the firm's own money, but the client is not usually entitled to interest on it.

Settlement Queue
In the CREST settlement system, the sequences, one for each stock and one for credit (cash) into which matched transactions are entered once the intended settlement date has been reached. Once the transactions are on the queue, CREST assesses whether or not the resources (stock and cash) are available to settle them.

Settlement Risk
See *Risk, Settlement*.

Settlor
The person who sets up a trust.

SFA
See *The Securities and Futures Authority*.

SFA Investigations Department
Responsible for investigating member firms who have been referred by the Monitoring Department for suspected misconduct.

Shape
The quantity of shares to be delivered by the seller to the buyer.(noun)
To split a bulk order into smaller constituent quantities.(verb)

Share
The unit of ownership of a company.

Share Capital
The figure on the balance sheet representing the nominal value of the shares that have been issued.

Share Certificate
A certificate issued by a company to a shareholder stating either that a named person is the registered owner or that the bearer is the owner.

Share Exchange Facility
A facility offered by some investment and unit trust managers to transfer an investor's existing shareholdings into a trust.

Share Premium Account
The figure in the balance sheet that represents the excess of the issue price of shares over the nominal value. US accounts use the term 'paid in surplus'.

Share Split
A split of one share into a number of shares with a smaller nominal value.

Share Yield
The share yield is a percentage of the quoted price of shares in an OEIC, representing the prospective annual income of the OEIC for its current annual accounting period, after deduction of all charges. The yield is expressed gross of tax.

Shareholder
The owner of a share in a company – the part–owner of a company.

Shareholder Insurance
Life assurance arrangements whereby shareholder directors in a small company take out policies which will pay out on the death of a shareholder director allowing the survivors to buy his shares.

Shareholders' Funds
The total of the share capital and the reserves of the company, shows how the shareholders have funded the company through subscribing for capital and through the retention of profits.

Shareholders' Rights
The legal rights of a shareholder such as the right to vote at meetings.

Short
Having an obligation to a buyer to deliver stock the seller does not already own.

Short Position
The result of a market maker selling shares or other securities which it does not have.

Short Selling
Selling stock that you do not own.

Short Termism
Allegation made against fund managers that they are traders on a short term basis and are not willing to hold them for the long term or to exert influence on management to improve corporate performance but prefer to sell the shares.

Short-dated Gilt
Gilts due to be redeemed within the next seven years.

Short-Term Securities
Securities with a maturity of less than 12 months.

SIB
See *Securities and Investments Board*.

Sight Deposits
Constituent of M2, the money supply measure, comprising current and all other instant access accounts.

Simple-Yield-to-Maturity
SYM accounts for the effect of the capital gain or loss on maturity of a bond as well as the current yield. Any capital gain or loss is assumed to be uniform over the life of the bond.

Simplified Defined Contribution Scheme (SDCS)
An occupational scheme fit to provide 'basic' benefits on a money purchase basis. The maximum contribution for each member is 17% of pensionable salary.

Single Currency Interest Rate Swap
An interest rate swap where the interest payments are exchanged in the same currency.

Single Pricing
Pricing system widely used outside the UK, where unit trusts quote only one price instead of a bid and offer price. A sales charge is usually added when units/shares are purchased.

Sinking Fund
Funds put aside by a borrower to buy back its bonds in the market for cancellation.

Small Business Investor
Customer of an investment business which is a business entity, but does not meet the size criteria to enable it to be classified as an ordinary business investor. It receives the same level of protection as a private customer.

Small Self-Administered Scheme (SSAS)
A self-administered occupational scheme, normally with less than 12 members subject to special conditions for approval. At least one of the trustees must be a pensioner trustee; the trustees' powers are restricted with respect to borrowing money and investing in certain residential and other property.

Soft Commissions
The process of giving advice or providing other services in return for guaranteed business.

Soft Commodities
Description given to commodities such as sugar, coffee and cocoa. Most contracts are traded through LIFFE since its merger with the former London Commodity Exchange (LCE).

Soft Currency
A currency whose exchange rate is falling against other currencies as demand is weak. See *Hard Currency*.

Sole Proprietor
A business owned and managed by one individual who has unlimited liability for the liabilities of the business.

Sole Trader
See *Sole Proprietor*.

SPAN
Standardised Portfolio Analysis of Risk. A form of margin calculation which is used by various clearing organisations. SPAN calculates the effect of a range of possible changes in volatility and price on derivative portfolios.

Special Cum
Terms of a bargain dealt during the ex period of a benefit distribution whereby the buyer receives the benefit entitlement, instead of the seller.

Special Ex
Terms of a bargain dealt during the cum period of a benefit distribution whereby the seller receives the benefit entitlement instead of the buyer.

Special Ex Date
The first date in the cum period from which special ex transactions can be agreed. It is set ten business days prior to the ex date.

Specialist
A type of dealer on the New York Stock Exchange responsible for ensuring an orderly market in a range of stocks.

Speculator
The speculator is a trader who wants to assume risk for potentially much higher rewards.

Split Capital Investment Trusts
'Splits' are special investment trusts created to separate different types of return of capital and income. All splits have pre-determined winding up dates. Income shares are normally entitled to receive all or most of the income of the underlying investments. Capital shares are normally entitled to all surplus assets on winding up. Zero dividend preference shares ('zeros') offer a pre-determined growth of capital over a fixed period, but no income.

Sponsored Member
Type of CREST member, usually a private investor, whose name appears on the company's share register but who has no computer link with CREST.

Spot Rate
The current exchange rate of a currency for delivery up to two business days after transaction date.

Spread
Difference between a market maker's buying (bid) and selling (ask) price.

SRO
See *Self Regulating Organisation*.

SSN
See *Stock Situation Notice*.

Stabilisation
A price supporting process used on new issues of securities or bonds in order to maintain the price at level which may otherwise not prevail.

Stag
Someone who applies for a new issue of shares intending selling them (at a profit) as soon as secondary market dealings start.

Stamp Duty
A UK tax on the physical transfer of certain certificated securities.

Stamp Duty Reserve Tax (SDRT)
A UK tax on the electronic transfer of certain securities (equities and convertible loan stocks).

Standard & Poor's 500
One of the Indexes of the New York Stock Exchange. See *Dow Jones Average*.

State-controlled economy
Country where all aspects of activity are controlled by the government.

Stepped Preference Shares
Share in a split capital trust which provides a pre-determined amount of growth and pays a dividend.

Stock
The US equivalent of a share.

Stock Borrowing and Lending Intermediary (SBLI)
An organisation authorised by the Inland Revenue to act as an intermediary between stock borrower (eg, market maker) and lender (eg, institution) to preserve anonymity. Formerly known as London Stock Exchange money broker.

Stock Deposit
A transaction (type STD) for the dematerialisation of certificated stock into a CREST member's account.

Stock Deposit Reference Number (SDRN)
A unique identifier on a CREST Transfer Form which links a stock deposit to its instruction in CREST.

Stock Dividend
See *Scrip dividends*.

Stock Exchange
An organisation that provides facilities for companies and governments to issue securities to raise money and for those securities to be traded among investors.

Stock Exchange Automated Quotation System (SEAQ)
Electronic screen display system through which market makers in equities display prices at which they are willing to deal.

Stock Exchange Electronic Trading System (SETS)
Computerised matching system through which traders in equities dis–play prices and quantities of stock they wish to buy or sell.

Stock Index Futures / Options
Based on the value of an underlying stock index like the FTSE 100 in the UK, the S & P 500 index in the US and the Nikkei 225 and 300 in Japan. Delivery is fulfiled by the payment or receipt of cash against the exchange calculated delivery settlement price. These are referred to as either indices or indexes.

Stock Lending
An activity whereby holders of shares or bonds lend them to traders or market makers to facilitate the settlement of bargains and increase efficiency in the market.

Stock Loan (Agreement) (SLO)
A CREST transaction which transfers a specified security, against payment, from one member to another. When the stock loan settles, pre–matched stock loan returns are automatically created.

Stock Loan Return (SLR)
A pre–matched CREST standard transaction created on settlement of a stock loan (SLO). It is created with a settlement date of the next business day, with a priority of zero.

Stock Queue
See *Settlement Queue*.

Stock Situation Notice (SSN)
A notice issued by the London Stock Exchange to advise member firms of the dates and details of a stock situation (corporate action).

Stock Transfer Form (STF)
Form defined by the Stock Transfer Act 1963 used to register the transfer of stock or registered securities from one name to another.

Stock Withdrawal (STW)
The transaction for changing dematerialised stock held in a CREST member's account to certificated stock.

Stockmarket
Description usually given to a stock exchange.

Straight Bond
A bond with a fixed coupon rate and no conversion or early redemption features.

Stratified Sampling
A method of setting up a tracker fund in which a sample of shares is held which, statistically, should perform like the index to be tracked.

Strike Price
Alternative term for the exercise price.

Stripped Bonds (Strips)
Bonds where the rights to the interest payments and eventual repayment of the nominal value have been separated from each other and trade independently. Facility introduced for gilts in December 1997.

Style classification
Methodology for classifying shares into certain investment style categories.

Sub–Agent
See *Sub–Custodian*.

Sub–Custodian
A bank which provides clearance and safekeeping services in its domestic market on behalf of a global custodian based overseas.

Subdivision
A corporate action in which a company decides to increase the number of issued shares whilst simultaneously reducing the nominal value of each share so as to leave the total nominal value of the issued capital unchanged. For example, if a company replaces each share with two new shares, the value of each new share will be half that of the old. Sometimes called a 'stock split'.

Subordinated Loan Stock
A special type of loan stock which ranks after the other creditors, but before shareholders.

Subscription (exercise of warrants)
A corporate action in which holders of warrants may exercise their right to subscribe for ordinary shares in the company by exercising the warrant. Although warrants may be attached to other securities, they are usually detached, and traded as a separate line of stock. If not exercised by the final subscription date, the warrants lapse.

Subsidiary
A company, at least 50% of which is owned by another company. See Holding Company.

Suitability
The appropriateness of investments considering a customer's attitude to risk, and financial and investment objectives.

Sum Assured
The amount payable under a life policy.

SuperDot
Computer dealing system of the New York Stock Exchange.

Surrender Value
The encashment value of a life policy before it becomes a claim by maturity or death.

Suspense Account
Account where client money is held if there are no clear instructions on which bank account to credit.

Swap
Arrangement where two borrowers, one of whom has fixed interest and one of whom has floating rate borrowings, swap their commitments with each other. A bank would arrange the swap and charge a fee. Commodity, currency, equity and interest rate swaps are all commonly traded.

SWIFT
The Society for Worldwide Interbank Financial Telecommunication was founded in 1973 to service the payments needs of the banking industry through standardised, electronic messages. The securities markets became involved in 1987 with the acceptance of stock exchanges, brokers and depositories into the SWIFT network. Also, SWIFT is one of the approved CREST Network providers.

Switch
Sale of one stock and subsequent reinvestment into another stock.

Switching Discount
A discount, normally expressed as a percentage reduction in the offer price, given to investors upon switching from one fund to another within the same group.

SYCOM
The overnight trading system operated by the Sydney Futures Exchange (SFE).

Syndicate
A group of securities houses who are placing a new issue of eurobonds under the authority of a lead manager.

Syndicated Issue
An issue method whereby new securities are sold to the clients of syndicate banks.

Syndicated Loan
A loan by a number of financial institutions to one borrower for a predetermined term and at a margin over short–term interest rates.

Syntegra
One of the approved CREST network providers, the systems integration business of British Telecom plc.

T

T+3
Settlement takes place three business days after the date of the transaction.

T+5
Settlement takes place five business days after the date of the transaction.

TII
See *Treasury Inflation Indexed securities*.

Takeover
When one company obtains more than 50% of another company's shares.

Takeover Panel
See *Panel on Take Overs and Mergers*.

Talisman
The Stock Exchange computerised settlement system which was fully replaced by CREST in April 1997.

Talon
See *Coupon*.

Tap
A sale of a government instrument eg. a bond or treasury bill in response to demand.

Tap Stock
A government bond which is issued in varying amounts at different times.

TARGET
The Trans–European Automated Real–Time Gross Settlement Express Transfer system that will handle the settlement of cross border payments of the Euro

Tariffable Unit (TU)
The unit of charging for CREST transactions (TU), based on the cost charged by CRESTCo to each counterparty for a movement of stock and cash between two memberships, with CREST matching input from both counterparties (ie, a standard stock/cash delivery (DEL)).

Tax Avoidance
The legal use of tax concessions to reduce or dispose of a tax charge or debt.

Tax Claims
Interim Claim (PEP10): Form on which the plan manager claims back from the Inland Revenue the tax which has been deducted at source (at 20%) from the net dividends and distributions received on holdings in a PEP. Interim claims may be made monthly (in tax months 6th–5th). *Annual Claim* (PEP14): The formal claim for all tax credits and adjustments for the whole of a complete tax year, subject to audit by the plan manager's external auditors.

Tax Credit
Income distributions, whether paid or reinvested, are treated as the top slice of income and carry a tax credit of 20%. A tax credit voucher is usually issued with the dividend or interest payment. Investors liable to tax at the basic rate or lower rate band will have no further liability to tax. Higher rate taxpayers will have a further liability to tax. Non-taxpayers can use the tax credit voucher to support a tax repayment claim. To be phased out by the government.

Taxable Income
The total income in a year less allowances available at the marginal rate.

Tax Year
The tax year runs from 6 April to the following 5 April.

Technical Analysis
Analysis of past and current share prices in order to make investment decisions on the basis of trends in those prices. See *Charts*.

Technical Standards Committee (TSC)
The body recognised by BSI and ISO as representing practitioners in the UK Securities Industry in the setting of national and international standards in so far as they apply to the industry.

Term
The length of time that a security has until it matures or its value can be redeemed.

Term Assurance
A policy that pays out only if death occurs within a certain period. There is no savings element.

Term Loan
An advance by a financial institution for a given period, which has to be repaid, with interest, at regular intervals.

Terminal Bonus
A bonus paid on death or maturity of a with–profits policy.

Tested Telex
A telex message bearing a code number, for authentication purposes, calculated in accordance with a test key.

Theoretical Value
The price of an option (or future) as computed by a mathematical model. If the assumptions used in the model are accurate then this will equate to the 'fair' value.

Three–tier Approach
System devised by SIB to be more flexible than the original regulatory framework. It comprises 10 general principles as Tier 1, 40 core rules as Tier 2 and detailed rules and codes of conduct written by individual SROs as Tier 3. This System ceased in November 1994 with the de–designations of Tier 2 rules.

Tick Value
The value of a one point movement (0.01 per cent) in the price of an exchange trade financial future or option.

Tied Agent
An individual or business which only sells one company's products (such as life assurance) rather than advising independently on all the products available.

Time decay
The rate at which the time value of an option deteriorates over its life.

Time Value
The portion of an options price that is not its intrinsic value.

Timely Execution
To execute a client's order at a time that is in the best interests of the customer.

Title
The right to ownership and enjoyment of property.

Tokyo Stock Exchange
The Tokyo Exchange is the second largest (after NYSE) and is predominantly an order–driven market.

Tom Next
A transaction with value dates for tomorrow against the next day.

Top–down Management
A method of active portfolio management where different classes of security (cash, bonds, shares) are selected; then within each class different sectors are selected; and within each sector individual securities are selected.

Touch
The best prices available for a stock on the stockmarket, looking at all market makers.

Tracker Fund
A unit trust which invests in the companies which comprise a Stock Exchange index so as to follow the movements of the index.

Trade Confirmation
The process by which the two counterparties to a trade input their instructions to a central system which compares them and, if the instructions agree, confirms them and passes them on for settlement.

Trade Customer
A small business or small trust who applies to change its status from Private Customer to Non–private Customer.

Trade Date
The date on which an order to buy or sell a security is executed.

Traded Option
A term that usually refers to options dealt on a recognised exchange.

Tradepoint
RIE established in 1995 as a rival to the London Stock Exchange. Uses an order–driven matching system.

Trading Permits
These are issued by exchanges and give the holder the right to have one trader at any one time trading in the contract(s) to which the permit relates.

Transaction
Usually refers to the order to purchase or sell a security or to receive or pay cash.

Transaction Date
See *Trade Date*.

Trans–European Automated Real–Time Gross Settlement Express Transfer (TARGET)
See *TARGET*.

Transfer Form
Document which owners of registered securities must sign when they sell the security. Not required where a book entry transfer system is in use.

Transfer Value
The amount trustees pay to another pension scheme or an insurance company for an early leaver. They are capital sums intended to represent the present value of future pension benefits. Transfer values may be paid to a new employer's scheme, a Section 32 buy-out bond or a personal pension plan.

Transparent
A description of a market where investors have full immediate knowledge of the details of trades taking place.

TRAX
ISMA's real time confirmation and risk management system used by brokers, market makers, institutional investors and fund managers to confirm trades in bonds and other securities.

Treasury
Arm of Government responsible for all financial decisions and regulation of the financial services sector.

Treasury Bills
Short term government securities which pay no interest so are issued at a discount. Also known as T-bills and usually have a maturity of 91 days.

Treasury Bonds
Coupon bearing government securities with a maturity date greater than 5 years. Also known as T-bonds.

Treasury Inflation Indexed Securities
Securities issued by the US government.

Treasury Notes (US)
US government bond issued with 2,3,5 and 7 year maturity. Also known as T–notes.

Triple–A rating
The highest credit rating for a bond or company where the risk of default (or non–payment) is negligible. See *AAA rating*.

Trust
An arrangement whereby people called trustees hold property for the benefit of others called the beneficiaries.

Trust Deed
The legal document drawn up between the trustees and the managers containing basic details of the constitution of a unit trust.

Trustee
A person or organisation who is the owner of assets held in trust. Responsible for safeguarding the assets, monitoring compliance with the trust deed and the activities of the trust manager.

Trustee Investments Act, 1961
This Act laid down certain requirements which a security must meet before it can be bought by trustees. The object of the Act allowed trustees to invest in equity shares, giving their beneficiaries the prospect of capital growth.

TSC
See *Technical Standards Committee*.

Turn
See *Spread*.

Two–way Customer Agreements
A document, which must be signed by the client, outlining the contractual obligations between a Stock Exchange member firm and its client.

Two–way Price
Simultaneous prices in a stock quoted by a market maker, the lower at which he is willing to buy and the higher at which he is willing to sell.

U

Uberrima Fides
Utmost good faith.

UCITS
A European Directive governing 'Undertakings for Collective Investment in Transferable Securities'. It is designed to harmonise the operation of collective investment schemes which includes authorised unit trusts throughout the European Community, with a view to facilitating the sale of funds in other member states.

Ultra Vires
Outside the legal powers of an official or company.

Umbrella Funds
A single authorised unit trust scheme with any number of constituent parts, providing the opportunity for unit holders to switch all or part of their investment from one part to another. Each part may have an entirely separate portfolio.

Unauthorised Unit Trust
A unit trust which does not comply with FSA's criteria to make it authorised and which can only be marketed to sophisticated investors.

Uncertificated Transactions
Transactions involving dematerialised stock held in CREST.

Uncovered Sale
Selling an option without possessing the wherewithal to meet the obligations implicit in that sale. The writer of a call who does not possess the stock is said to be uncovered, as is the writer of a put who has no cash or near cash to pay for stock.

Undated Stock
An interest bearing security, usually issued by the British Government, which has no final date of repayment of the principal sum.

Underlying
The financial instrument on which an option or future is based, sometimes referred to as 'the cash'.

Underlying Instrument
The instrument on which a futures or options contract is based.

Undersubscribed
Circumstance when people have applied for fewer shares than are available in a new issue.

Underwriters (of a share or bond issue)
Institutions which agree to take up shares in a new issue if it is undersubscribed. They will be paid an underwriting fee.

Underwriting (Insurance)
The procedure of assessing a risk and deciding whether to accept it and at what premium.

Underwriting Agreement
An agreement between the lead manager and the underwriters setting out the terms and obligations of each party to the agreement.

Underwriting Fee
The fee paid to institutional investors who agree to underwrite a new issue of securities.

Unfranked Income
Unfranked income carries no ACT tax credit. All sterling bonds except prefs are deemed to be paying loan interest and so the interest is paid net of basic income tax, but the gross interest that the issuing company pays will be considered for tax purposes and could result in a further tax liability or refund to the company.

Unfunded Pension Scheme
A pension scheme where pensions are paid out of the current profits of the company.

Unit Trust
A unit trust is a means of allowing an individual investor to participate in a large portfolio of shares with many other investors. Identical units are sold each representing a small fraction of the portfolio. As the number of units grows, the underlying portfolio is increased.

Unit Trust Association (UTA)
The former name of trade association for the unit trust industry now known as AUTIF. See *AUTIF.*

Unit Trust Yield
The yield is a percentage of the quoted offer price of a unit trust, representing the prospective annual income of the trust fund for its current annual accounting period, after deducting all charges. The yield is expressed gross of tax.

Unitised With–Profits
With–profits investments expressed as unit–linked policies. Benefits are based on unit holdings rather than on the sum assured payable at maturity or death.

Unit–Linked Policy
A policy where the value is linked to the value of units in a fund run by a life office or units of a unit trust. The units directly reflect values of the underlying assets of the fund. Whole of life, endowment, permanent health insurance and even term assurance policies may be unit–linked.

Universal Whole Of Life Policy
Unit–linked whole of life policies with a wide range of benefits including death, accidental death, permanent disability, critical illness, permanent health insurance.

Unlisted Company
A company whose shares are not listed on the stock exchange. See *Alternative Investment Market*.

Unmatched Transaction
The result of an instruction not matching in CREST because: either only one party input a transaction instruction; or, although both parties input instructions, one or more of the matchable fields did not match. Certain types of transactions in CREST do not require matching.

Unrealised Profit
A profit which arises from the revaluation of an asset but where there is no actual sale.

Unsecured Loan Stocks
Domestic bonds which are not secured on any assets of the borrower.

Unsolicited Call
A personal visit or oral communication made without the recipient's express invitation.

Up Tick
The last trade in a share is at a price higher than the one before.

V

Value Added Tax (VAT)
A general tax on goods and services which was introduced into the UK in 1973.

Value Date
The date on which cash is credited to or debited from an account. It has the same meaning as settlement date.

Vanilla Swap
Two parties enter into an agreement to exchange the difference between a fixed rate of interest and a nominated floating rate.

Variation Margin
Debits and credits on a margin account arising once a portfolio has been marked to market. Variation margin is calculated at the end of each business day by LCH.

Venture Capital
Funds provided by, for instance, a bank, building society or specialised lending institution to an individual to start up or develop a business or company where a high degree of risk may be involved.

Vertical Spread
A combination of options, where one option is purchased and another is sold, both with the same expiry date. The spread will be a constructed with either calls or puts.

Volatility
A measure of how much an underlying instrument is likely to fluctuate (or has fluctuated in the past) during a defined time period. See *Historic* and *Implied Volatility*.

Vostro
Italian for "your" usually associated with accounts maintained by foreign banks held by other banks in another currency and country. The opposite to Nostro.

Voting Shares
Shares which entitle a holder to vote in the election of directors of a company.

W

Warning
A non-mandatory warning given to a member firm by the SFA Investigations Department where an abuse is either discovered or thought likely to occur.

Warrant
An equity warrant offers the holder the right to buy underlying equity at a predetermined price on specified dates, or at any time, up to the end of a predetermined time period. A warrant differs from an option in that options usually have a life of less than 1 year. Warrants are usually issued by companies or by securities houses and have a life span of more than 1 year. The exercise of a company–issued warrant will result in an increase of the capital of that company.

Weekly Official Intelligence (WOI)
Weekly publication by the London Stock Exchange which provides (amongst other things) a summary of company announcements during that week.

Whole Life Assurance
A life policy which pays out on death, whenever it occurs.

Winding Up
See *Liquidation*.

Window Dressing
Financial adjustments by companies for the purposes of accounting representation. A company may, for instance, raise a short–term loan in order to show their balance sheet in a favourable light.

Wire Transfer
A type of payment where the clearing house debits the participant's cash account and pays the funds externally to the beneficiary's account held by another bank See *Book Transfer*.

Withholding Tax (WHT)
Tax deducted from dividends on investments which are paid to foreign investors. This can be claimed back if there is a Double Taxation Agreement in place between the two countries

With–Profits
Policies where policyholders receive a guaranteed sum assured plus a share of the investment profits of the life fund in the form of bonuses.

Working Capital
Net current assets.

Working Member
A broker or underwriter who carries out the actual business (as a professional member) at Lloyd's of London.

World Bank
See *International Bank for Reconstruction and Development*.

Writer
The seller of an option (usually refers to an opening sale). See *Holder*.

X

XD
See *Ex–dividend*

Y

Yankee Bond
A US dollar bond issued in the US by a non–US issuer eg. a foreign bank.

Yellow Book
See *Listing Rules*.

Yield
The yield on an investment is the interest or dividend income as a percentage of the capital value. This is also known as the running yield. The yield to redemption also takes into account the annualised capital profit (or loss) on holding a fixed interest security to redemption, ie the investors have an annual average total return.

Yield Curve
A series of interest rates plotted against the time to maturity to which they apply. The graph below show the 'normal' shape of a yield curve.

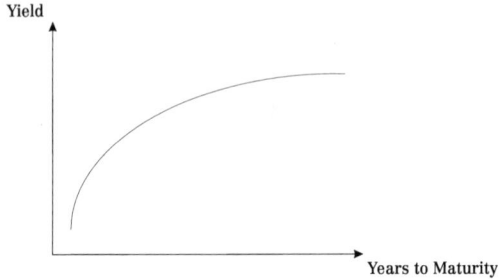

Yield to Maturity
See *Gross Redemption Yield*.

Z

Zero Coupon Bonds
A deep discount bond where the coupon payable per annum is zero and the entire return of the bond is in the form of capital accrual from the original discounted price to the final redemption value at maturity of the bond.

Zero Dividend Preference Shares
Issued by split capital investment trusts these shares pay no income but promise to repay the shares at a higher level at a fixed date. The shares are very tax efficient and are frequently used for school fees planning.

SECURITIES INSTITUTE PUBLISHING

Securities Institute Publishing

Each publication provides a detailed overview and practical introduction to key topics within financial services.

The two titles in our *Essential Elements* series – EMU and Money Laundering – provide rapid briefing on key issues as they arise. Each booklet contains the relevant facts and figures to give you an overview of the subject.

Our *Griffin Guide* range consists of re-worked and updated notes from our popular courses. These publications are a useful reference for everyone who needs to grasp the basics of a topic – fast!

Forthcoming publications include:

- Introduction to Financial Market Mathematics
- Introduction to Understanding and Interpreting Financial Statements
- Securities and Derivatives
- Products and Trading
- Custody, Stock Lending and Derivatives Clearing
- Operations Management
- Operational Risk Management

To place an order or find out more, call now on *0207 645 0680*.

SECURITIES INSTITUTE PUBLISHING

Essential Elements

Essential Elements of the Prevention of Money Laundering

This quick guide looks at the scale of the problem and efforts taken to overcome it: an essential reference for all who are concerned to identify attempts at money laundering within their organisation.

- What is money laundering?
- Money laundering and the law
- How do you spot it in the process, and what to do.

£4.99 32pp paperback, ISBN: 1 900520 36 2

The Essential Elements of Economic & Monetary Union

Economic and Monetary Union (EMU) is the system that links together the economies and currencies of the participating European countries. The European Central Bank has become responsible for centralised monetary policy. What does the Euro mean for you?

- Convergence
- Impact of the Euro on the markets
- Preparing for the future.

£4.99 28pp paperback, ISBN: 1 900520 31 1

SECURITIES INSTITUTE PUBLISHING

Griffin Guides

The Fundamentals of CREST

The Fundamentals of CREST gives a detailed overview of securities administration and settlement through the CREST system. It is illustrated throughout with diagrams and tables, bullet points and summaries.

- Handling Certificated Securities
- Corporate Actions and Claims
- Stock Loans and Collateral.

£11.99 96pp paperback, ISBN: 1 900520 06 0

An Introduction to Swaps

An Introduction to Swaps gives a detailed overview of how the various categories of swap work, how they are traded and what they are used for. Topics include interest rate swaps, managing risk, asset swaps, currency swaps. The book is illustrated with over 50 diagrams and tables.

- Managing risk with swaps
- Asset swaps
- Currency swaps.

£16.99 160pp paperback, ISBN: 1 900520 21 4

SECURITIES INSTITUTE PUBLISHING

An Introduction to Fund Management

An Introduction to Fund Management introduces readers to the economic rationale for the existence of funds, the different types available, investment strategies and many other related issues from the perspective of the investment manager. Topics include the features and characteristics of funds, portfolio management and administration, performance measurement and investment mathematics. Includes relevant formulae, equations and examples.

- Features and characteristics of funds
- Portfolio management and administration
- Performance measurement
- Investment mathematics.

£16.99 160pp paperback, ISBN: 1 900520 61 3

An Introduction to Value–at–Risk

An Introduction to Value–at–Risk has been written for those with little or no previous understanding of or exposure to the concepts of risk management and Value–at–Risk. Topics include applications of VaR, instrument structures, stress testing, VaR for corporates, credit risk and legal/regulatory issues.

- Risk and Risk management
- VaR and Derivatives, Fixed Interest products.

£16.99 176pp paperback, ISBN: 1 900520 66 4

SECURITIES INSTITUTE PUBLISHING

Introduction to Equity Markets

Introduction to Equity Markets provides an overview of the current financial services industry. The book introduces the reader to different types of companies and shares as well as analysis of UK markets. An overview of dealing and settlement in some of the world's major markets is also featured. Contents include:

- Shareholders and Company Law
- Issuing Shares – The Primary Market
- Trading Shares – The Secondary Market
- Settlement of Transactions
- Major Overseas Exchanges and Indices
- Dividends, Bonus Issues and Rights Issues
- Company Accounts.

£16.99 170pp paperback, ISBN: 1 900520 71 0

Introduction to Bond Markets

Introduction to Bond Markets provides a comprehensive, authoritative description and analysis of the bond markets. The book considers basic 'plain vanilla' bonds and elementary bond mathematics, before looking at the array of different instruments available. Contents include:

- Bond Yield Measurement
- Corporate Debt Markets
- Eurobonds
- Introduction to Repo
- Risk Management
- Off–Balance Sheet Instruments
- Government Bond Markets
- Emerging Bond Markets.

£16.99 410pp paperback, ISBN: 1 900520 81 8

SECURITIES INSTITUTE PUBLISHING

Introduction to the Gilt Strips Market

Introduction to the Gilt Strips Market provides a thorough description and analysis of gilt strips. The contents describe and define strips as a financial instrument and examine the use and application of gilt strips within the context of the capital markets as a whole. Contents include:

- Zero–coupon bonds
- The yield curve
- Interest rate risk for strips
- Settlement, tax and regulatory issues
- Trading and strategy

£16.99 192pp paperback, ISBN: 1 900520 91 5

Introduction to Repo Markets

An Introduction to Repo Markets provides a comprehensive description and analysis of the repo markets. The text has been written to cater for those with little or no previous experience of the repo markets, though it also develops the subject matter to sufficient depth to be of use to more experienced practitioners. Contents include:

- Uses and economic functions of repo
- Accounting, Tax and Capital issues
- The UK gilt repo market
- The implied repo rate and basis trading
- Repo and the yield curve

£16.99 240pp paperback, ISBN: 1 900520 86 9

SECURITIES INSTITUTE PUBLISHING

Dictionary of Financial and Securities Terms

This dictionary is intended to give a quick, clear and straight forward definition of frequently used terms in the financial and securities industry. Also included is a comprehensive listing of abbreviations and acronyms.

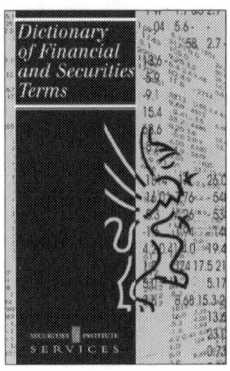

- What is a Bill of Exchange?
- What does SPAN stand for?
- What are CHIPS and CHAPS?
- What is the standard definition of EPS?

Approximately 1,500 entries. Included with the dictionary is a FREE CD–ROM version for users to load onto their PC for easy reference at home or at work.

£15.00 240pp paperback, ISBN: 1 900520 96 6

For further details on these and other new titles, contact Client Services Department on 0207 645 0680